100 LITERACY ASSESSMENT LESSONS

TERMS AND CONDITIONS

IMPORTANT – PERMITTED USE AND WARNINGS – READ CAREFULLY BEFORE USING

Licence

YEAR 3

Scottish Primary 4

Minimum specification:
- PC or Mac with a CD-ROM drive and 512 Mb RAM (recommended)
- Windows 98SE or above/Mac OS X.4 or above
- Recommended minimum processor speed: 1 GHz

For all technical support queries, please phone Scholastic Customer Services on 0845 603 9091.

Gillian Howell

CREDITS

Author
Gillian Howell

Development Editor
Niamh O'Carroll

Editors
Louise Titley and
Carolyn Richardson

Project Editor
Fabia Lewis

Series Designers
Joy Monkhouse and
Melissa Leeke

Designers
Sonja Bagley, Allison Parry and
Quadrum Ltd

Illustrations
Anna Godwin (unless
otherwise credited)

CD-ROM development
CD-ROM developed in
association with Vivid
Interactive

ACKNOWLEDGEMENTS

The publishers gratefully acknowledge permission to reproduce the following copyright material: **Catherine Benson** for the use of 'Cat Dream' by Catherine Benson from *Word Whirls and other shape poems* collected by John Foster © 1998, Catherine Benson (1998, Oxford University Press). **James Carter** for the use of 'Inside' from *Time-travelling Underpants* by James Carter © 2005, James Carter (2005, Pan Macmillan). **Sue Cowling** for the use of 'Lullaby' by Sue Cowling from *The Works 4* chosen by Pie Corbett and Gaby Morgan © 2005, Sue Cowling (2005, Macmillan). **David Higham Associates** for the use of an extract from *Someone's Watching, Someone's Waiting* by Jamila Gavin © 1998, Jamila Gavin (1998, Mammoth). **Jan Dean** for the use of 'It's not what I'm used to' by Jan Dean from *The Works 4* chosen by Pie Corbett and Gaby Morgan © 2005, Jan Dean (2005, Macmillan). **Peter Dixon** for the use of 'Where do all the teachers go?' from *Grow your own poems* by Peter Dixon © 1998, Peter Dixon (1998, Macmillan) and for 'Fairy Picnic' by Peter Dixon from *The Tortoise had a mighty roar* by Peter Dixon © 2005, Peter Dixon (2005, Macmillan). **Tony Langham** for the use of 'Autumn' by Tony Langham from *World Whirls and other shape poems* collected by John Foster © 1998, Tony Langham (1998, Oxford University Press). **Irene Rawnsley** for the use of 'Treasure Trove' by Irene Rawnsley from *Ask a silly question* by Irene Rawnsley © 1988, Irene Rawnsley (1988, Methuen Children's Books). **Rogers, Coleridge and White** for the use of 'Summer Farm' by Gareth Owen from *Collected Poems* by Gareth Owen © 2000, Gareth Owen (2000, Macmillan). **Kit Wright** for the use of 'The Magic Box' by Kit Wright from *Cat among the pigeons* by Kit Wright © 1987, Kit Wright (1987, Viking Kestrel).

Text © 2009, GIllian Howell
© 2009, Scholastic Ltd

Designed using Adobe
InDesign.

Published by Scholastic Ltd
Villiers House
Clarendon Avenue
Leamington Spa
Warwickshire CV32 5PR

Visit our website at
www.scholastic.co.uk

Printed by Bell and Bain Ltd

123456789 9012345678

Mixed Sources
Product group from well-managed
forests and other controlled sources
www.fsc.org Cert no. TT-COC-002769
© 1996 Forest Stewardship Council
FSC

Every effort has been made to trace copyright holders for the works reproduced in this book, and the publishers apologise for any inadvertent omissions.

British Library Cataloguing-in-Publication Data
A catalogue record for this book is available from the British Library.
ISBN 978-1407-10191-0

Contents

100 Literacy Assessment Lessons: Year 3

'Assessment' refers to all those activities undertaken by teachers, and by their students in assessing themselves, which provide information to be used as feedback to modify the teaching and learning activities in which they are engaged.'

from Black and William *Inside the Black Box*

About the series

100 Literacy Assessment Lessons is a response to the Assessment for Learning strategy (AfL) and Assessing Pupils' Progress (APP) and contains all new, stand-alone material. The lessons mirror the guidelines and viewpoints of the revised approach to assessment. The CD-ROMs provide appropriate and exciting texts and a variety of assessment activities from photocopiable pages for individual, whole-class or group work to stimulating interactive activities. Together, the books and CD-ROMs will be an invaluable resource to help you understand and implement the revised approach to assessment.

About assessment

The key points of the revised approach to assessment are as follows:
● Assessments are accurate and linked to National Curriculum levels;
● Assessments are targeted, with assessment focuses used as the guiding criteria;
● Assessments are reliable and based on a range of evidence;
● Assessments are useful and appropriate: day to day, periodic or transitional.

Type of assessment	Purpose	Strategies
Day to day	Ongoing and formative: encourages reflection and informs the next steps in teaching and learning.	Objectives, outcomes and success criteria are made explicit and are shared with children; observations are used to gather evidence; peer assessment and self-assessment help to develop children as responsible learners.
Periodic	Provides a periodic view of children's progress and diagnostic information linked to national standards.	Progress and attainment are reviewed regularly (half-termly or termly) against APP criteria; strengths and gaps in learning are identified to inform future planning.
Transitional	Brings together evidence, including tests, at points of transition (eg level to level or year to year); provides a formal overview of children's attainment set within the framework of national standards.	Use of formal tasks and tests; external validation and reporting.

For a complete list of strategies for day-to-day assessment and further information about periodic and transitional assessment, visit the National Strategies website (**http://nationalstrategies.standards.dcsf.gov.uk**).

What are assessment focuses (AFs)?

Assessment focuses (AFs) are tools for assessment that sit between the National Curriculum programmes of study and level descriptions. The AFs provide more detailed criteria against which children's standards of attainment can be assessed and judged.

About the book

Reflecting the structure of the renewed Primary Framework for Literacy (2006), the book is divided into three Blocks: Narrative, Non-fiction and Poetry. Each Block is further divided into Units, and the Units are split into Phases. The Phases are divided into a number of day-to-day assessment activities. These assessment activities, based on learning outcomes, are designed to fit easily into your existing planning.

Units

Each Unit covers a different text-type or genre and, because of this, each Unit has its own introduction containing the following:

Literacy objectives: All objectives for the Unit are listed under their strand names.

Key aspects of learning: Aspects of learning that the Unit covers are identified from the renewed Primary National Strategy (PNS) Framework.

Assessment focuses (AFs): The main assessment focuses that are addressed during the Unit are listed from APP.

Speaking and listening: Assessment areas you should look out for are linked to the Speaking and listening strand objectives.

Resources: Lists all of the resources required for the activities in each Phase.

Planning grids: There are two grids per Unit to provide an overview of the Unit and to suggest how you can build assessment opportunities into your medium-term planning. The grids show Phases, learning outcomes, a summary of lessons, assessment opportunities and potential evidence, levelled statements of the assessment focuses (AFs), and success criteria matched to the learning outcomes in the form of 'I can...' statements.

Assessment activities

Each assessment activity follows the same format:

Learning outcomes: These are relevant to individual activities or a set of activities that share objectives.

Success criteria: These are child-friendly 'I can...' statements for children or teachers to refer to during or following the activity.

Setting the context: This section provides guidance on what the task is and details the children's expected prior learning. The context for the task may also be explained: group, paired or individual work. Where adult support is required, this is also described.

Assessment opportunity: This section highlights what to assess, how to find out what children know, and what questions to ask.

Assessment evidence: This section suggests what to look for during an activity in relation to specific assessment focuses (AFs).

Next steps: This section is divided into support and extension. It provides ideas to enable children to revisit an objective or learning outcome, and gives feedback or targets to move children forward, consolidate or extend their learning.

Key aspects of learning: Key aspects of learning are linked to specific activities.

Photocopiable pages

At the end of each Unit is a selection of photocopiable activity pages. The full range of these is provided on the CD-ROM, including levelled versions where appropriate. Photocopiable pages may include self-assessment statements for ticking as well as a 'traffic light' system for colouring (see 'Self-assessment' on page 7 for more information.) Where 'I can...' statements are not included, peer assessment may be suggested within an activity.

Transitional assessment

Also included on the CD-ROM are some SATs-style formal single-level assessments. More information about these can be found on page 7, and a grid detailing their content is provided on page 174.

How to use the materials

The activities in the book provide a balance of whole-class/group/paired/ independent learning and teaching, and give the opportunity not only for day-to-day assessment but also for collection of evidence against individual assessment focuses (AFs) for periodic review. Each activity can be slotted into a lesson where appropriate and may involve discussion work, written responses, use of photocopiable pages or interactive activities.

Two periodic assessment activities are provided at the end of each Unit – one for reading and one for writing. The focus of each of these activities is usually a photocopiable page that assesses children on the learning outcomes covered during the Unit and provides further evidence against the assessment focuses. You can also use these periodic assessments to help you to make level judgements that match to the Reading and Writing Attainment Targets (ATs).

Making a level judgement

Assessment involves making a level judgement against national standards at regular intervals. The following steps will support you in adopting a strategic approach to the marking and levelling needed for assessment.

Step one: Consider evidence
- Use a range of appropriate evidence to make a level judgement, for example, written or oral;
- Remember that it is quality not quantity that matters;
- Keep examples of children's work that will provide significant evidence.

Step two: Review the evidence
- Take a broader view of a child's achievement across the whole subject and over time;
- Create a visual picture of strengths and learning gaps by highlighting criteria a child has met across a range of evidence;
- Collaborate with colleagues and agree what constitutes success for the various assessment criteria.

Step three: Make a judgement
- Consult the English Assessment Guidelines (see National Standards website: **http://nationalstrategies.standards.dcsf.gov.uk** and look at exemplar material provided in the Standards files;
- Arrive at an overall subject level judgement;
- Think about what the child demonstrates:
  - How much of the level;
  - How consistently;
  - How independently;
  - In what range of contexts.
- Finally, fine-tune your levelling to 'high', 'secure' or 'low'.

What's on the CD-ROM?

Each CD-ROM contains a wealth of resources. These include:
- **Photocopiable pages:** levelled where appropriate, including text extracts and activity sheets for day-to-day and periodic assessment.
- **Transitional assessments:** single-level tests for levels 2–5 including mark schemes and instructions.
- **Interactive activities:** for individuals or small groups, with in-built marking to assess specific learning outcomes.
- **Whiteboard tools:** a set of tools (including a pen, highlighter, eraser, notes and reward stickers) that can be used to annotate activity sheets or interactive activities. These tools will work on any interactive whiteboard or conventional screen.
- **Editable planning grids** (in Word format) are available to help teachers integrate the assessment activities into their medium-term and weekly planning.

How to use the CD-ROM

System requirements

Minimum specification:

- PC or Mac with a CD-ROM drive and 512 Mb RAM (recommended)
- Windows 98SE or above/Mac OS X.4 or above
- Recommended minimum processor speed: 1 GHz

Getting started

The *100 Literacy Assessment Lessons* CD-ROM should auto run when inserted into your CD drive. If it does not, browse to your CD drive to view the contents of the CD-ROM and click on the *100 Literacy Assessment Lessons* icon.

From the start-up screen you will find four options: select **Credits** to view a list of acknowledgements. Click on **Register** to register the product in order to receive product updates and special offers. Click on **How to use this CD-ROM** to access support notes for using the CD-ROM. Finally, if you agree to the terms and conditions, select **Start** to move to the main menu.

For all technical support queries, contact Scholastic Customer Services help desk on 0845 6039091.

Navigating the CD-ROM

The CD-ROM allows users to search for resources by Block or Unit, or by assessment focus. Users can also search by assessment type (day to day, periodic or transitional) or by resource type (for example, worksheet, interactive resource, or text extract).

Day-to-day assessments

These should be used to support learning. They can be used during a lesson, when you judge that children are ready for an assessment activity. The materials can also be used weekly or after a unit of work has been completed.

Periodic assessments

These can be used with a group of children rather than with the whole class. This could be at the end of a unit of work (for example, at the end of a half-term or term). Decide who is ready to be assessed using the outcomes of the day-to-day assessment activities and your observations of children's performance.

Self-assessment

There is a 'traffic light' system at the bottom of some photocopiable pages that children can shade to show how they feel about the activity: red for 'need help'; orange for 'having some understanding'; green for 'I found this easy!'. (Alternatively, you may wish to utilise these as a teacher marking tool for providing an at-a-glance guide to the child's progress.)

The photocopiable sheets also provide 'I can…' statements with tick boxes, to enable children to self-assess specifically in terms of the relevant learning outcomes/success criteria. A similar system is in place at the end of all the interactive activities, where the children are asked to click on a traffic light, and to type in any comments.

Transitional tests

These single-level tests provide evidence of where, in relation to national standards, children are at a given point in time. There are two Reading and Writing assessments for each level. Each reading assessment consists of a two-part reading comprehension test based on two different text types. Each writing assessment consists of two writing tasks – shorter and longer – that focus on writing for different purposes. All the tasks and tests for levels 2–5 are included on the CD-ROM together with easy-to-follow marking schemes (see pages 174–175 for more information.)

Class PET

A whole-school version of *100 Literacy Assessment Lessons* is available with an expanded range of digital assessment activities, as well as the facility to report, record and track children's work. For further information visit the Class PET website, **www.scholastic.co.uk/classpet**.

Periodic assessment

Unit	AT	Page	Assessment focuses	Learning outcomes
Narrative 1	Reading	24	AF2, AF3, AF5, AF6	Children can form opinions of a text and use evidence.
	Writing	25	AF1, AF7	Children can compose and punctuate a series of sentences to describe a familiar setting.
Narrative 2	Reading	44	AF2, AF3, AF5, AF6	Children can identify the main features of a quest myth, including the introduction of the main characters, the problem to be overcome, the journey undertaken and the resolution to the problem.
	Writing	45	AF1, AF3	Children can write a complete quest myth organised into a clear sequence of events.
Narrative 3	Reading	61	AF2, AF3, AF5, AF6	Children can identify key features of adventure stories. Children can identify how the author engages the reader and maintains interest.
	Writing	62	AF3	Children can write an extended adventure story with logically sequenced events and resolution.
Narrative 4	Reading	76	AF5	Children can identify the key features of different types of letter.
	Writing	76	AF2	Children can explain why they like books by a particular author referring to an author's style or themes.
Narrative 5	Reading	90	AF1, AF2, AF4	Children can explain how the use and conventions of written dialogue differ between prose and playscripts.
	Writing	91	AF1	Children can understand the conventions and features of playscript writing.
Non-fiction 1	Reading	106	AF4	Children can recognise the structure and language features of a non-chronological report.
	Writing	107	AF1-8	Children note information from reading more than one source and present it in the form of a non-chronological report.
Non-fiction 2	Reading	117	AF4	Children can recognise the structure and language features of instructional text.
	Writing	117	AF2, AF3	Children can write an instructional text using selective adverbial language, sequenced imperative statements and presentational features such as bullet points and numbering.

Periodic assessment

Unit	AT	Page	Assessment focuses	Learning outcomes
Non-fiction 3	Reading	132	AF4	Children can recognise the features and purpose of simple persuasive texts, recounts, non-chronological reports and instructions.
	Writing	133	AF2	Children can use notes collected from a range of sources and present them in different forms, including ICT, and evaluate their effectiveness.
Poetry 1	Reading	143	AF5, AF6	Children can explain their opinions about a poem by referring to particular words and phrases and the subject of the poem. Children can identify where language is used to create an effect.
	Writing	144	AF1, AF7	Children can write a poem that uses language to create an effect.
Poetry 2	Reading	156	AF5, AF6	Children can explain what they like about a poem by referring to particular words and phrases and the subject of the poem.
	Writing	157	AF1, AF2	Children can write a calligram, choosing appropriate presentational features using ICT to create effects, and can describe why these effects have been chosen.
Poetry 3	Reading	169	AF5, AF6	Children can recognise how poets use language to create a vivid picture in words.
	Writing	170	AF1, AF7, AF8	Children can write poems that use poetic images in different forms.

PERIODIC

NARRATIVE

UNIT 1 Stories with familiar settings

Literacy objectives

Speak and listen for a wide range of purposes in different contexts

Strand 1 Speaking
- Sustain conversation, explain or give reasons for their views or choices.

Strand 2 Listening and responding
- Follow up others' points and show whether they agree or disagree in whole-class discussion.

Strand 4 Drama
- Use some drama strategies to explore stories or issues.

Read and write for a range of purposes on paper and on screen

Strand 7 Understanding and interpreting texts
- Explore how different texts appeal to readers using varied sentence structures and descriptive language.

Strand 8 Engaging with and responding to texts
- Share and compare reasons for reading preferences, extending the range of books read.
- Identify features that writers use to provoke readers' reactions.

Strand 9 Creating and shaping texts
- Select and use a range of technical and descriptive vocabulary.

Strand 11 Sentence structure and punctuation
- Compose sentences using adjectives, verbs and nouns for precision, clarity and impact.

Strand 12 Presentation
- Write with consistency in the size and proportion of letters and spacing within and between words, using the correct formation of handwriting joins.
- Develop accuracy and speed when using keyboard skills to type, edit and re-draft.

Key aspects of learning

Reasoning
- Children will ask questions about the reasons for events in stories.

Evaluation
- Children will discuss criteria for their written work, give feedback to others and judge the effectiveness of their own descriptions.

Empathy
- Writing and listening to stories based on first-hand experiences will help children to understand what others might be thinking or feeling in a particular situation.

Social skills
- When working collaboratively, children will listen to and respect other people's ideas. They will undertake a variety of roles in group contexts.

Communication
- Children will develop their ability to discuss as they work collaboratively in paired, group and whole-class contexts. They will communicate outcomes orally, in writing and through ICT if appropriate.

Assessment focuses

Reading
AF5 *(explain and comment on writers' use of language, including grammatical and literary features at word and sentence level).*
AF6 *(identify and comment on writers' purposes and viewpoints, and the overall effect of the text on the reader).*

Writing
AF1 *(write imaginative, interesting and thoughtful texts).*
AF5 *(vary sentences for clarity, purpose and effect).*
AF7 *(select appropriate and effective vocabulary).*

Speaking and listening
Speaking (speak with clarity, intonation and pace).
Listening and responding (ask relevant questions and respond appropriately).
Drama (plan, perform and evaluate plays).

Resources

Phase 1
Photocopiable page, 'Senses used in stories'
Phase 2
Photocopiable page, 'The dark wood'
Interactive activity, 'Atmospheres'
Photocopiable page, 'Problems
Interactive activity, 'Problems'
Photocopiable page, 'Develop the setting' (versions 1 and 2)
Phase 3
Image, 'Playground setting'
Photocopiable page, 'Playground setting' (versions 1 and 2)
Photocopiable page, 'Opening a story'
Photocopiable page, 'Imaginative vocabulary'
Interactive activity, 'Improve a setting description'
Photocopiable page, 'Improve a setting description' (versions 1 and 2)
Periodic assessment
Photocopiable page, 'Narrative 1 Reading assessment text'
Photocopiable page, 'Narrative 1 Reading assessment'
Photocopiable page, 'Narrative 1 Writing assessment'
Recommended texts
The Mousehole Cat by Antonia Barber (ISBN 978-0744-52353-9)
The Colour of Home by Mary Hoffman (ISBN 978-0711-21991-5)
Harriet's Hare by Dick King-Smith (ISBN 978-0440-86340-3)
Boy by James Mayhew (ISBN 978-0439-65106-6)
Red Eyes at Night by Michael Morpurgo (ISBN 978-0340-68753-6)
Someone's Watching, Someone's Waiting by Jamila Gavin (ISBN 978-0749-73106-9)

Unit 1 📖 Stories with familiar settings

Learning outcomes	Assessment opportunity and evidence	Assessment focuses (AFs)		Success criteria
		Level 2	Level 3	
Phase ① activities pages 15-16				
Responding to a setting Children can express views clearly as part of a group discussion.	• Supported group discussion of story setting descriptions. • Notes on children's oral responses.	**Reading AF5** • Some effective language choices noted. • Some familiar patterns of language identified.	**Reading AF5** • A few basic features of writer's use of language identified, but with little or no comment.	I can listen and respond.
Senses used in stories Children can form opinions of a text and use evidence.	• Supported group discussion of children's preferred story setting descriptions. • Children's oral and written responses.	**Reading AF6** • Some awareness that writers have viewpoints and purposes. • Simple statements about likes and dislikes in reading, sometimes with reasons.	**Reading AF6** • Comments identify main purpose. • Express personal response but with little awareness of writer's viewpoint or effect on reader.	• I can draw comparisons between two stories. • I can form opinions of a story and give reasons.
Phase ② activities pages 17-19				
Atmospheres Children can use visual elements to write sentences describing settings.	• Supported group activity where children write sentences to describe story settings. • Children's oral responses, completed interactive activities and photocopiables.	**Reading AF5** • Some effective language choices noted. • Some familiar patterns of language identified.	**Reading AF5** • A few basic features of writer's use of language identified, but with little or no comment.	I can choose alternative vocabulary to change the atmosphere of a text.
Problems Children can use visual elements to write sentences describing settings.	• Supported group activity where children write sentences to describe story settings. • Children's completed interactive activities and notes on their oral responses.	**Writing AF1** • Mostly relevant ideas and content, sometimes repetitive or sparse. • Some apt word choices create interest. • Brief comments, questions about events or actions suggest viewpoint.	**Writing AF1** • Some appropriate ideas and content included. • Some attempt to elaborate on basic information or events. • Attempt to adopt viewpoint, though often not maintained or inconsistent.	I can create a problem for a character.
Develop the setting Children can use visual elements to write sentences describing settings.	• Supported group activity where children write sentences to describe story settings. • Children's completed photocopiable pages.	**Writing AF1** • Mostly relevant ideas and content, sometimes repetitive or sparse. • Some apt word choices create interest. • Brief comments, questions about events or actions suggest viewpoint.	**Writing AF1** • Some appropriate ideas and content included. • Some attempt to elaborate on basic information or events. • Attempt to adopt viewpoint, though often not maintained or inconsistent.	I can develop a description of a setting.
Phase ③ activities pages 20-23				
Playground setting Children can compose and punctuate a series of sentences to describe a familiar setting.	• Supported group activity where children write three sentences to describe a setting. • Children's written responses on the photocopiable page.	**Writing AF1** • Mostly relevant ideas and content, sometimes repetitive or sparse. • Some apt word choices create interest. • Brief comments, questions about events or actions suggest viewpoint.	**Writing AF1** • Some appropriate ideas and content included. • Some attempt to elaborate on basic information or events. • Attempt to adopt viewpoint, though often not maintained or inconsistent.	• I can explore images. • I can write sentences using the senses to describe a setting.

Unit 1 ▣ Stories with familiar settings

Learning outcomes	Assessment opportunity and evidence	Assessment focuses (AFs)		Success criteria
		Level 2	Level 3	
Opening a story Children can compose and punctuate a series of sentences to describe a familiar setting.	• Supported group activity where children write a story opening. • Children's completed photocopiable pages.	**Writing AF5** • Some variation in sentence openings. • Mainly simple sentences with *and* used to connect clauses. • Past and present tense generally consistent.	**Writing AF5** • Reliance mainly on simply structured sentences, variation with support. • *and, but, so* are the most common connectives, subordination occasionally. • Some limited variation in use of tense and verb forms, not always secure.	I can write an opening sentence.
Imaginative vocabulary Children can compose and punctuate a series of sentences to describe a familiar setting.	• Supported group activity where children note down adjectives and adverbs for their story settings. • Children's completed photocopiable pages and paired responses.	**Writing AF7** • Simple, often speech-like vocabulary conveys relevant meanings. • Some adventurous word choices.	**Writing AF7** • Simple, generally appropriate vocabulary used, limited in range. • Some words selected for effect or occasion.	I can make notes.
Improve a setting description Children can compose and punctuate a series of sentences to describe a familiar setting.	• Paired activity where children choose adjectives/adverbs to improve their setting descriptions. • Children's completed interactive activity and notes on children's responses.	**Writing AF7** • Simple, often speech-like vocabulary conveys relevant meanings. • Some adventurous word choices.	**Writing AF7** • Simple, generally appropriate vocabulary used, limited in range. • Some words selected for effect or occasion.	I can improve a setting description.

Learning outcomes	Assessment opportunity and evidence	Assessment focuses (AFs)		Success criteria
		Level 4	Level 5	
Phase ① activities pages 15–16				
Responding to a setting Children can express views clearly as part of a group discussion.	• Independent group discussion of story setting descriptions. • Children's discussions and notes of oral responses.	**Reading AF5** • Some basic features of writer's use of language identified. • Simple comments on writer's choices.	**Reading AF5** • Various features of writer's use of language identified, with some explanation. • Comments show some awareness of the effect of writer's language choices.	I can listen and respond.
Senses used in stories Children can form opinions of a text and use evidence.	• Independent group discussion of story setting descriptions. • Individual written responses.	**Reading AF6** • Main purpose identified. • Simple comments show some awareness of writer's viewpoint. • Simple comment on overall effect on reader.	**Reading AF6** • Main purpose clearly identified, often through general overview. • Viewpoint in texts clearly identified, with some, often limited, explanation. • General awareness of effect on the reader, with some, often limited, explanation.	• I can draw comparisons between two stories. • I can form opinions of a story and give reasons.
Phase ② activities pages 17–19				
Atmospheres Children can use visual elements to write sentences describing settings.	• Independent activity where children write sentences to describe story settings. • Children's oral responses and completed interactive activity.	**Reading AF5** • Some basic features of writer's use of language identified. • Simple comments on writer's choices.	**Reading AF5** • Various features of writer's use of language identified, with some explanation. • Comments show some awareness of the effect of writer's language choices.	I can choose alternative vocabulary to change the atmosphere of a text.

Unit 1 🔲 Stories with familiar settings

Learning outcomes	Assessment opportunity and evidence	Assessment focuses (AFs)		Success criteria
		Level 4	Level 5	
Problems Children can use visual elements to write sentences describing settings.	• Independent activity where children write their own ideas of problems for a character in particular setting. • Children's written responses on the photocopiable page and notes on their oral responses.	**Writing AF1** • Relevant ideas and content chosen. • Some ideas and material developed in detail. • Straightforward viewpoint generally established and maintained.	**Writing AF1** • Relevant ideas and material developed with some imaginative detail. • Development of ideas and material appropriately shaped for selected form. • Clear viewpoint established, generally consistent, with some elaboration.	I can create a problem for a character.
Develop the setting Children can use visual elements to write sentences describing settings.	• Independent activity where children write sentences to describe story settings. • Children's written responses on the photocopiable page.	**Writing AF1** • Relevant ideas and content chosen. • Some ideas and material developed in detail. • Straightforward viewpoint generally established and maintained.	**Writing AF1** • Relevant ideas and material developed with some imaginative detail. • Development of ideas and material appropriately shaped for selected form. • Clear viewpoint established, generally consistent, with some elaboration.	I can develop a description of a setting.

Phase ③ activities pages 20–23

Learning outcomes	Assessment opportunity and evidence	Level 4	Level 5	Success criteria
Playground setting Children can compose and punctuate a series of sentences to describe a familiar setting.	• Independent activity where children write six sentences to describe a setting. • Children's written responses.	**Writing AF1** • Relevant ideas and content chosen. • Some ideas and material developed in detail. • Straightforward viewpoint generally established and maintained.	**Writing AF1** • Relevant ideas and material developed with some imaginative detail. • Development of ideas and material appropriately shaped for selected form. • Clear viewpoint established, generally consistent, with some elaboration.	• I can explore images. • I can write sentences using the senses to describe a setting.
Opening a story Children can compose and punctuate a series of sentences to describe a familiar setting.	• Independent group activity where children write a story opening. • Children's completed photocopiable pages.	**Writing AF5** • Some variety in length, structure or subject of sentences. • Use of some subordinating connectives throughout the text. • Some variation, generally accurate, in tense and verb forms.	**Writing AF5** • A variety of sentence lengths, structures and subjects provides clarity and emphasis. • Wider range of connectives used to clarify relationship between ideas. • Some features of sentence structure used to build up detail or convey shades of meaning.	I can write an opening sentence
Imaginative vocabulary Children can compose and punctuate a series of sentences to describe a familiar setting.	• Independent activity where children note down adjectives and adverbs for their story settings. • Children's completed photocopiable pages and paired responses to vocabulary choices.	**Writing AF7** • Some evidence of deliberate vocabulary choices. • Some expansion of general vocabulary to match topic.	**Writing AF7** • Vocabulary chosen for effect. • Reasonably wide vocabulary used, though not always appropriately.	I can make notes.
Improve a setting description Children can compose and punctuate a series of sentences to describe a familiar setting.	• Independent activity where children choose adjectives/adverbs to improve their setting descriptions. • Children's completed interactive activity.	**Writing AF7** • Some evidence of deliberate vocabulary choices. • Some expansion of general vocabulary to match topic.	**Writing AF7** • Vocabulary chosen for effect. • Reasonably wide vocabulary used, though not always appropriately.	I can improve a setting description.

NARRATIVE

Phase ① Responding to a setting

Learning outcome
Children can express views clearly as part of a group discussion.

Success criteria
I can listen and respond.

Setting the context
This activity should be carried out once the children have explored several contrasting settings with a focus on the senses of sight, sound, smell and touch. Select an extract from a story that uses the senses in a setting description. Suitable stories might include *Harriet's Hare* by Dick King-Smith, *The Colour of Home* by Mary Hoffman or *The Mousehole Cat* by Antonia Barber. Read the extract aloud to the children two or three times. The children will then identify which senses are used in the text during a group discussion.

Assessment opportunity
Children working at levels 2–3 work in supported discussion groups. Remind the children which senses are usually used to describe a setting in a story. Read the extract and ask questions to check they recognise the use of the senses. For example, if using the text *Harriet's Hare,* questions to ask could include: *Why do you think Harriet woke up suddenly?* (She heard a noise.) *Which sense is this?* (Sound/hearing.) *How is the noise described?* (It is compared to a rocket on Guy Fawkes Night.) Children working at levels 4–5 will work in small independent groups to identify any descriptions that use the senses of sound, sight, touch or smell. They will discuss how they feel about the setting and why. They will then report their findings orally and explain what effect the use of the senses has on them as readers.

Assessment evidence
At levels 2–3, children will spot basic features of the language and, with the help of the adult's prompts, will recognise the use of the senses. Children working at levels 4–5 will identify and make comments on the author's choice of language, focusing particularly on the use of the senses to describe the setting. Use the notes taken during this discussion activity to provide evidence for Reading AF5.

Next steps
Support: For those children who seem reluctant to contribute their own responses to the text, give them opportunities to name the sense used in a short section or phrase. Encourage and praise their response.
Extension: Ask children to create an anthology of effective setting descriptions from their reading that make good use of the senses. They should include their responses to the text, such as how it makes them feel.

Key aspects of learning
Social skills: When working collaboratively, children will listen to and respect other people's ideas.
Communication: Children will develop their ability to discuss as they work collaboratively in paired, group and whole-class contexts. They will communicate outcomes orally.

NARRATIVE

Phase ① Senses used in stories

Learning outcome
Children can form opinions of a text and use evidence.

Success criteria
- I can draw comparisons between two stories.
- I can form opinions of a story and give reasons.

Setting the context
This activity should be undertaken after the children have discussed and analysed several different setting descriptions. Ask them to think about the setting in a story they are reading independently and to describe the setting to the class. Remind the children about the work they have done on the use of senses in setting descriptions and use the class novel and their own personal reading to make notes to compare both settings using the prompts on photocopiable page 'Senses used in stories'.

Assessment opportunity
Children working at levels 2–3 will work in a supported group. Ask questions about the children's personal reading to prompt them to think about the setting of their story and the class novel, for example, *What does the main character see when the story opens? What do the characters hear? Which senses are used in both stories? Which story uses the sense of feeling? Which setting do you prefer? Can you give me a reason why?* After discussion the children can complete the photocopiable page independently. Children working at levels 4–5 will complete the photocopiable prompt sheet independently.

Assessment evidence
At levels 2–3, children will make simple statements about their own likes and dislikes. At levels 4–5, children will show more awareness of each author's viewpoint and the effects of their choice of language. These children will be able to explain their personal preferences, and give reasons for them. Use the children's completed sheets as evidence for Reading AF6.

Next steps
Support: For children who struggled to give reasons for their preferences, provide a selection of adjectives and phrases from which to choose, to help them articulate their opinions. Emphasise that, when expressing a personal opinion about a text, there is no right or wrong answer.
Extension: After personal reading, ask the children to recommend something they are reading to the rest of the class, giving reasons for their opinions.

Key aspects of learning
Social skills: When working collaboratively, children will listen to and respect other people's ideas.
Communication: Children will develop their ability to discuss as they work collaboratively in paired, group and whole-class contexts. They will communicate outcomes orally, in writing and through ICT if appropriate.

NARRATIVE

Phase ② Atmospheres

Learning outcome
Children can use visual elements to write sentences describing settings.

Success criteria
I can choose alternative vocabulary to change the atmosphere of a text.

Setting the context
This activity should be undertaken after the children have analysed several different setting descriptions and explored vocabulary that creates an atmosphere in a setting. Read together the sentences on the photocopiable page 'The dark wood'. Discuss the atmosphere created in the description of the dark wood. Ask the children to say which words create the mood and how they feel about the setting. Children then choose alternative vocabulary to change the atmosphere to a bright or happy setting using the interactive activity 'Atmospheres'.

Assessment opportunity
Children working at levels 2–3 work in a supported group to read the sentences together before completing the activity. Children may also use the photocopiable page while doing the activity to help them eliminate wrong choices. After the children have completed the activity, ask them to give reasons for their choices and make notes against the class list of individual responses. The children working at levels 4–5 read the sentences on the photocopiable page independently before completing the interactive activity 'Atmospheres'.

Assessment evidence
At levels 2–3 children will choose appropriate but simple vocabulary but they will find it difficult to give reasons for their choices. At levels 4–5 children will use more imaginative vocabulary and will show an awareness of its possible effects on the reader. They will explain why they have chosen particular words. Use the children's oral responses and completed activities to provide evidence for Reading AF5.

Next steps
Support: Ask children to describe the mood or atmosphere of the stories they are reading in class and to find words or phrases that create this atmosphere.
Extension: Ask children to use the sentences on the photocopiable page to write an extended description of the setting of 'The dark wood'.

Key aspects of learning
Social skills: When working collaboratively, children will listen to and respect other people's ideas.
Communication: Children will develop their ability to discuss as they work collaboratively in paired, group and whole-class contexts. They will communicate outcomes orally, in writing and through ICT if appropriate.

NARRATIVE

Phase ② Problems

Learning outcome
Children can use visual elements to write sentences describing settings.

Success criteria
I can create a problem for a character.

Setting the context
This activity should be undertaken after the children have analysed different setting descriptions and the various problems met by main characters in these settings. Discuss the settings on the photocopiable page 'Problems'. Ask the children to say what sort of problems characters might encounter in each of them. They then choose a problem for each setting from the list of options and undertake the interactive activity 'Problems'. They should select one of the settings and write, on their whiteboards, an extended description of the problem for a main character.

Assessment opportunity
Mask the list of options for children working at levels 4–5 and ask them to write their own ideas of problems for a character in each of the settings. Children working at levels 2–3 work in a supported group and discuss which problem best suits each setting. An adult working with the supported group can ask questions to draw out and deepen the children's responses, for example: *What might the character on a spacecraft want badly?* (For example, he might have run out of fuel and need to find some.) *Why would this be difficult to achieve? How would the character solve the problem? What might happen to a character in a fairytale castle?* (For example, he or she might be threatened by an evil character.) *How could this problem be solved? What might someone lose in a playground or at the seaside? What would he or she do to try and find it again?*

Assessment evidence
At levels 2–3 children will generate some appropriate ideas and content but these may be repetitive or sparse. Children working at levels 4–5 will develop and shape their ideas more effectively, using imaginative detail to flesh out the characters and their problems. Use the children's completed interactive activities and notes made on the class list of children's oral responses to provide evidence for Writing AF1.

Next steps
Support: Send different stories home each day for a week and ask children to summarise the problems met by the main characters.
Extension: Children develop the problem and make notes of how the character overcomes the problem.

Key aspects of learning
Reasoning: Children will ask questions about the reasons for events in stories.
Social skills: When working collaboratively, children will listen to and respect other people's ideas.
Communication: Children will develop their ability to discuss as they work collaboratively in paired, group and whole-class contexts. They will communicate outcomes orally, in writing and through ICT if appropriate.

Phase ② Develop the setting

Learning outcome
Children can use visual elements to write sentences describing settings.

Success criteria
I can develop a description of a setting.

Setting the context
This activity should be undertaken after the children have contributed to shared writing and collaborated in writing a class story. Write the beginning of a setting description on the board during a shared writing opportunity, or use an enlarged copy of the photocopiable page 'Develop the setting' (version 2). Discuss the text with the children and ask them to suggest how the description could continue. Remind them that there is no right or wrong answer, but that they can continue the description to make it their own piece of writing. Ask the children to continue the setting description from their own imaginations by writing three more sentences.

Assessment opportunity
Provide children working at levels 2–3 with version 1 of the photocopiable page 'Develop the setting', which includes hints at the bottom of the page. Arrange them to work in a supported group to discuss details they could add to the setting. An adult working with the supported group can ask questions to draw out and deepen their responses, for example: *Where do you think this setting is?* (The seaside.) *How do you know this?* (The text mentions sand, sea and the tide. The text describes how the sand feels.) *What else might the author feel?* (For example, the wind...) *Add a sentence that uses a description of the wind. The author sees shining brown mud. What else might he/she see?* Children working at levels 4–5 continue the setting description independently on version 2 of the photocopiable page.

Assessment evidence
Children working at levels 2–3 will generate some appropriate ideas and content but these may be repetitive or sparse. Children working at levels 4–5 will develop and shape their ideas more effectively, using imaginative detail to describe and develop the setting. Use both the completed photocopiable pages and the children's independent writing as evidence for Writing AF1.

Next steps
Support: Help children who struggled to add descriptive details from their own imaginations to the setting description, to generate descriptive vocabulary using a thesaurus and add it to their writing journals.
Extension: Children develop the setting description by writing a paragraph of more than three sentences.

Key aspects of learning
Social skills: When working collaboratively, children will listen to and respect other people's ideas.
Communication: Children will develop their ability to discuss as they work collaboratively in paired, group and whole-class contexts. They will communicate outcomes orally, in writing and through ICT if appropriate.

NARRATIVE

Phase ③ Playground setting

Learning outcome
Children can compose and punctuate a series of sentences to describe a familiar setting.

Success criteria
● I can explore images.
● I can write sentences using the senses to describe a setting.

Setting the context
Display the image 'Playground setting' from the CD-ROM. Discuss the image with the children and ask them to describe what they see. Then ask them to suggest what they might hear and feel in the setting. Using the children's suggestions, model writing a sentence to describe the setting using more than one sense, for example: *The children's voices rose and fell as they ran across the hot playground.* Point out that the sentence uses sound (children's voices) and feeling (hot) to describe the setting. Ask the children to write a setting description of three or more sentences using the image from the CD-ROM.

Assessment opportunity
Distribute versions 1 and 2 of the photocopiable page 'Playground setting'. Children working at levels 2–3 work in a supported group using version 1. Children should write notes of what they can see, hear and feel using the image 'Playground setting' from the CD-ROM as a stimulus, then compose three sentences. The adult working with the supported group can ask questions to draw out and deepen their responses, for example: *You have written 'The playground is hot'. Could you add another sense to that sentence?* (For example, 'noisy'.) *How can you add 'noisy' to the sentence?* (For example, 'The noisy playground is hot.') Children working at levels 4–5 should write six sentences and include more than one of the senses in some of the sentences, using version 2 of the photocopiable page.

Assessment evidence
At levels 2–3 children will use relevant ideas and content, incorporating the occasional interesting or unusual word. Children working at levels 4–5 will maintain a more consistent authorial viewpoint and use more imaginative detail, developing and shaping their ideas more effectively. Use the children's written responses to provide evidence for Writing AF1.

Next steps
Support: For those children who struggled to compose and punctuate their sentences, ask them to compose a sentence orally, scribe it for them and then ask them to punctuate it.
Extension: Children develop their three sentences into a paragraph to give a more complete setting description.

Key aspects of learning
Social skills: When working collaboratively, children will listen to and respect other people's ideas.
Communication: Children will develop their ability to discuss as they work collaboratively in paired, group and whole-class contexts. They will communicate outcomes orally, in writing and through ICT if appropriate.

Phase ③ Opening a story

Learning outcome
Children can compose and punctuate a series of sentences to describe a familiar setting.

Success criteria
I can write an opening sentence.

Setting the context
Collect a selection of books with familiar settings that use different ways to open the story, including those that use a setting description to open the story, for example: Mary Hoffman's *The Colour of Home* begins with a classroom setting; *Boy* by James Mayhew begins in a cold cave; and *Red Eyes at Night* by Michael Morpurgo opens with a character description. Run this activity when the children have had the opportunity to immerse themselves in a variety of story openings, including in modelled and shared writing sessions on story openings. Provide the children with copies of the photocopiable page 'Opening a story' and ask them to write three to six sentences to open a story using the ingredients on the page.

Assessment opportunity
Children working at levels 2–3 should work in a small supported group of two to three using one copy of the photocopiable page. The adult working with the supported group can ask questions to stimulate their imaginations, for example: *Who is going to be in this story? Shall we give them names? What can they see?* (For example, they can see a table and two chairs.) *Can they see anything else? Imagine the boy and girl have just walked into the kitchen. What does the cat do when they come in? How can we write that as the first sentence?* To assess children working at levels 2–3, read both the collaborative story opening and the comments written on the class list by the adult helper. Children working at levels 4–5 should work independently to write up to six sentences, and should include more than one sense in some of the sentences.

Assessment evidence
At levels 2–3, children will write sentences that are simple in structure and correctly punctuated. At levels 4–5, children will write sentences that are more varied in structure, length and subject. Use this activity to provide evidence for Writing AF5.

Next steps
Support: Give other lists of different opening ingredients to practise with at home to those children who struggled to compose their story opening in small groups.
Extension: Allow the children to continue the story opening and write a complete story.

Key aspects of learning
Social skills: When working collaboratively, children will listen to and respect other people's ideas.
Communication: Children will develop their ability to discuss as they work collaboratively in paired, group and whole-class contexts. They will communicate outcomes orally, in writing and through ICT if appropriate.

Phase ③ Imaginative vocabulary

Learning outcome
Children can compose and punctuate a series of sentences to describe a familiar setting.

Success criteria
I can make notes.

Setting the context
This activity should be undertaken when the children have explored and collected imaginative words and phrases, adjectives and adverbs to use in story writing. Ensure that all children know about the function of adjectives and adverbs. They should have experienced shared and modelled writing sessions that focus on different ways of making notes when planning a story. Provide the children with copies of photocopiable page 'Imaginative vocabulary', a spidergram outline, and ask them to write notes of descriptive words and phrases to use for a story in a school setting. They then use some of their choices to write a sentence to describe an aspect of the setting.

Assessment opportunity
Children working at levels 2-3 will work in a supported group, each with a copy of photocopiable page 'Imaginative vocabulary'. The adult working with the supported group can ask questions to deepen their responses, for example: *You have made a note of 'teacher'. What adjectives could you add to describe the teacher?* (For example, strict, busy, kindly, angry...) *You have written 'playground'. How could you describe the playground?* (For example, cold and windy, noisy and crowded). *Can you think of a sentence that uses these two groups of words?* Ask the children to swap notes with a partner and identify two good vocabulary choices and one that could be improved. Children working at levels 4-5 will work independently to write notes on the spidergram on the photocopiable page and add other legs to it if required. They will write a sentence to describe an aspect of the setting using two of their descriptive words and phrases.

Assessment evidence
Children working at levels 2-3 will generate appropriate vocabulary - including the occasional adventurous word. They will be unable to substantiate their views on their classmates' vocabulary. Children working at levels 4-5 will choose more effective vocabulary. They will comment clearly on their partner's choices, explaining the reasons behind their remarks. Use the children's written responses and notes made by the group helper to provide evidence for Writing AF7.

Next steps
Support: Let those who struggled to make notes of imaginative vocabulary use a thesaurus to find alternative adjectives and adverbs and add these to their reading journals.
Extension: Children use their notes to write a paragraph about the setting using descriptive adjectives and adverbs.

Key aspects of learning
Evaluation: Children will discuss criteria for their written work, give feedback to others and judge the effectiveness of their own descriptions.
Social skills: When working collaboratively, children will listen to and respect other people's ideas.
Communication: Children will develop their ability to discuss as they work collaboratively in paired, group and whole-class contexts. They will communicate outcomes orally, in writing and through ICT if appropriate.

NARRATIVE

Phase ③ Improve a setting description

Learning outcome
Children can compose and punctuate a series of sentences to describe a familiar setting.

Success criteria
I can improve a setting description.

Setting the context
This activity should be undertaken when the children have written first drafts of setting descriptions and revised and improved them. They should have experienced shared and modelled writing sessions that focus on editing and improving writing. Ensure the children have had opportunities to explore the use of adjectives and adverbs to enhance and improve their writing. On the interactive activity 'Improve a setting description' the children read two screens with spaces for missing words and choose from a selection of adjectives and adverbs to enhance the setting description. This enables the children to make their own judgements about vocabulary choices as there are no right or wrong answers.

Assessment opportunity
Children working at levels 2–3 work in pairs and discuss the choices to reach joint decisions. Alternatively, individual children can work with a supporting adult and give reasons for their vocabulary choices. The adult can ask questions to enhance the child's response, for example: *What would the sentence sound like if you used 'angry' here? Try a different word and see if it sounds better.* The supporting adult can make notes of the child's responses. Children working at levels 4–5 make choices of adjectives and adverbs to enhance the setting description independently. This provides an opportunity to evaluate their personal judgements.

Assessment evidence
Supported by discussion and/or adult prompting, children working at levels 2–3 will choose words from the suggestions provided that are appropriate to the description. Children working at levels 4–5 will draw on the wider range of their own vocabulary, deliberately choosing words for their effect – even though their choices may not always be the best. This activity provides evidence for Writing AF7.

Next steps
Support: Provide children with version 1 of the photocopiable page, 'Improve a setting description' with a reduced number of word choices for those who struggled to make choices between the vocabulary given on the interactive activity, and ask them to fill in the gaps.
Extension: Use version 2 of the photocopiable page, 'Improve a setting description'. Children use the sheet to fill in the gaps with vocabulary choices of their own. Encourage them to continue the setting description.

Key aspects of learning
Evaluation: Children will discuss criteria for their written work, give feedback to others and judge the effectiveness of their own descriptions.
Social skills: When working collaboratively, children will listen to and respect other people's ideas.
Communication: Children will develop their ability to discuss as they work collaboratively in paired, group and whole-class contexts. They will communicate outcomes orally, in writing and through ICT if appropriate.

NARRATIVE

Periodic assessment

Reading

Learning outcome Children can form opinions of a text and use evidence.	**Success criteria** ● I can retrieve and interpret information from a text. ● I can comment on an author's use of language.

Setting the context

This assessment should be carried out once children have completed Narrative Unit 1. Give each child a copy of the photocopiable page, 'Narrative 1 Reading assessment text' (a setting description from *Someone's Watching, Someone's Waiting* by Jamila Gavin) and ask them to answer ten questions about it. The question types range from literal, about the subject and vocabulary, to evaluative, about the impression the setting gives. Read the extract aloud to the children before providing them with their copy of the photocopiable page 'Narrative 1 Reading assessment'. In order to pre-empt any problems in their understanding of the passage, identify any new, unusual or difficult vocabulary in the text, for example, *scuttling, straggled, torsos, muscular, exhilaration.* Ask them to re-read the passage carefully. Tell them to annotate any language features that strike them before reading the questions. Explain that doing this will help them to answer the questions.

Assessment opportunity

Give children time to read, digest and annotate the description before answering the questions. Encourage children working at levels 2–3 to explain their answers orally while you make notes. Assess the children's ability to understand the author's use of language and the overall effectiveness of the description.

Assessment evidence

At levels 2–3, children will answer the questions by eliciting specific facts that can be obtained from a literal interpretation of the text. They will identify but not comment on the features of the language used, and their awareness of the author's viewpoint will be limited. At levels 4–5, children will clearly identify textual features. They will interpret accurately the language used and the writer's purpose in using it and may make inferences and deductions from it. This assessment will provide evidence for Reading AF2, AF3, AF5 and AF6. Use this activity as well as examples of children's learning throughout this unit to help you make level judgements for Reading.

Periodic assessment

Writing

Learning outcome
Children can compose and punctuate a series of sentences to describe a familiar setting.

Success criteria
I can write a setting description.

Setting the context
This assessment should be carried out once children have completed Narrative Unit 1. Give each child a copy of the photocopiable page, 'Narrative 1 Writing assessment' and ask them to write three or more sentences to make a setting description. Remind the children of the work they have completed during the unit, about using vocabulary to create an atmosphere, using imaginative adjectives, verbs and adverbs and using the senses of sight, sound, smell and feeling. Encourage them to write notes of ideas before they begin writing.

Assessment opportunity
Give the children sufficient time to allow them to think of and make notes on ideas before beginning the activity. Assess the children's understanding of the work they have completed during the course of the unit and their ability to put it into practice to create effective setting descriptions.

Assessment evidence
At levels 2–3, children will use simple but appropriate vocabulary and occasionally choose words for their specific effects; ideas and content will also be appropriate but may be repetitive or sparse. Attempts to adopt a particular viewpoint may be inconsistent. At levels 4–5, children will use a wider vocabulary that matches the topic and is more deliberately chosen. Relevant ideas will be developed with more imaginative detail, establishing a clear and consistent viewpoint. This activity provides evidence for Writing AF1 and AF7. Use this activity as well as examples of children's work throughout this unit to make level judgements for Writing.

NARRATIVE

Name _____ Date _____

Senses used in stories

◼ How does the author use the senses to describe the settings in the book you are reading and the class novel?

I am reading _____

Sound: _____

_____

Sight: _____

_____

Feeling: _____

_____

The class novel _____

Sound: _____

_____

Sight: _____

_____

Feeling: _____

_____

Which setting do you like best and why?

_____

_____

Red
Amber
Green

I can draw comparisons between two stories. ☐

I can form opinions of a story and give reasons. ☐

Name	Date

Develop the setting (1)

■ Continue the setting description.

The sand felt hot and grainy under his bare feet. The tide was out and a wide stretch of shining brown mud lay between him and the water.

_____

_____

_____

_____

_____

_____

_____

_____

_____

_____

Hints:

What else can he feel? What can he hear? What else can he see?

Illustration © 2009, Anna Godwin.

Red
Amber
Green

I can develop a description of a setting.

NARRATIVE

Name   Date

Opening a story

Story ingredients

Write three or more sentences to open your story.

_____

_____

_____

_____

_____

_____

Red
Amber
Green   I can write an opening sentence. ☐

Name		Date

Improve a setting description (1)

■ Select words from the box to fill in the gaps.

wet	angry	huge	quickly	suddenly
old	heavy	sodden	violent	

The _____ wind whipped the branches of the

trees and sent showers of _____ leaves through

the air.

They _____ ran for shelter beneath a

_____ _____ oak.

The rain _____ became _____

and turned the _____ ground into mud.

A _____ crack of lightning lit up the forest.

Red ◯
Amber ◯   I can improve a setting description. ☐
Green ◯

NARRATIVE
Unit 2 Myths and legends

Literacy objectives

Speak and listen for a wide range of purposes in different contexts

Strand 3 Group discussion and interaction
- Use talk to organise roles and action.
- Actively include and respond to all members of the group.

Read and write for a range of purposes on paper and on screen

Strand 8 Engaging with and responding to texts
- Identify features that writers use to provoke readers' reactions.

Strand 9 Creating and shaping texts
- Use beginning, middle and end to write narratives in which events are sequenced logically and conflicts resolved.

Strand 10 Text structure and organisation
- Signal sequence, place and time to give coherence.

Strand 11 Sentence structure and punctuation
- Show relationships of time, reason and cause through subordination and connectives.

Key aspects of learning

Reasoning
- Children will predict and anticipate events in their own quest myth based on the actions of key characters and settings, using the language of cause and effect.

Evaluation
- Children will express their own views and preferences against agreed criteria to evaluate the work of others.

Empathy
- Writing and listening to stories will help children to understand what others might be thinking or feeling in a particular situation.

Social skills
- When working collaboratively, children will listen to and respect other people's ideas. They will undertake a variety of roles in group contexts.

Communication
- Children will develop their ability to discuss aspects as they work collaboratively in paired, group and whole-class contexts. They will communicate outcomes orally, in writing and through ICT if appropriate.

Assessment focuses

Reading
AF2 *(understand, describe, select or retrieve information, events or ideas from texts and use quotation and reference to text).*
AF3 *(deduce, infer or interpret information, events or ideas from texts).*
AF7 *(relate texts to their social, cultural and historical contexts and literary traditions).*

Writing
AF1 *(write imaginative, interesting and thoughtful texts).*
AF3 *(organise and present whole texts effectively, sequencing and structuring information, ideas and events).*
AF7 *(select appropriate and effective vocabulary).*

Speaking and listening
Group discussion and interaction (support others, take turns).

Resources

Phase 1
Photocopiable page, 'Different genres'
Interactive activity, 'Different genres'
Photocopiable page, 'Features of a quest myth' (versions 1 and 2)
Photocopiable page, 'Heroes and villains'
Interactive activity, 'Heroes and villains'
Phase 2
Photocopiable page, 'Develop the setting'
Image, 'Develop the setting'
Photocopiable page, 'Telling the story'
Interactive activity, 'Telling the story'
Phase 3
Photocopiable page, 'Write an opening' (versions 1 and 2)
Interactive activity, 'Character descriptions'
Periodic assessment
Photocopiable page, 'Narrative 2 Reading assessment text'
Photocopiable page, 'Narrative 2 Reading assessment'
Photocopiable page, 'Narrative 2 Writing assessment'

Unit 2 ◻ Myths and legends

Learning outcomes	Assessment opportunity and evidence	Assessment focuses (AFs)		Success criteria
		Level 2	Level 3	
Phase ① activities pages 35-38				
Different genres Children can identify the main features of a quest myth.	● Supported group activity where children match story titles to their genre. ● Children's responses to the interactive activity and notes on their oral responses.	**Reading AF7** ● General features of a few text types identified. ● Some awareness that books are set in different times and places.	**Reading AF7** ● Some simple connections between texts identified. ● Recognition of some features of the context of texts.	I can identify genres of stories.
Features of a quest myth Children can identify the main features of a quest myth.	● Supported group activity where children discuss and identify features of a quest myth. ● Children's written responses and notes on their oral responses.	**Reading AF2** ● Some specific, straightforward information recalled. ● Generally clear idea of where to look for information.	**Reading AF2** ● Simple, most obvious points identified though there may also be some misunderstanding. ● Some comments include quotations from or references to text, but not always relevant.	I can identify features of a quest myth.
Heroes and villains Children can identify the main features of a quest myth.	● Supported group activity where children discuss and identify heroes and villains. ● Notes on children's oral responses and the completed interactive activity.	**Reading AF3** ● Simple, plausible inference about events and information, using evidence from text. ● Comments based on textual cues, sometimes misunderstood.	**Reading AF3** ● Straightforward inference based on a single point of reference in the text. ● Responses to text show meaning established at a literal level or based on personal speculation.	I can identify heroes and villains from myths.
Create a character Children can identify the main features of a quest myth.	● Supported group activity where children create a hero and a villain for a quest story. ● Children's written responses and notes on their oral responses.	**Writing AF7** ● Simple, often speech-like vocabulary conveys relevant meanings. ● Some adventurous word choices.	**Writing AF7** ● Simple, generally appropriate vocabulary used, limited in range. ● Some words selected for effect or occasion.	I can plan elements for a quest story.
Phase ② activities pages 39-41				
Develop the setting ● Children can question others to find out further detail about a narrative. ● Children can tell a story orally, organised in a clear sequence.	● Supported, paired activity where children explore journeys using a story map of a quest myth. ● Peer-assessment. ● Notes on children's oral responses.	**Writing AF3** ● Some basic sequencing of ideas or material. ● Openings and/or closings sometimes signalled.	**Writing AF3** ● Some attempt to organise ideas with related points placed next to each other. ● Openings and closings usually signalled ● Some attempt to sequence ideas or material logically.	● I can discuss ideas with a partner, and describe our ideas to others. ● I can question others to find out about their ideas.
Group maps ● Children can question others to find out further detail about a narrative. ● Children can tell a story orally, organised in a clear sequence.	● Supported group activity where children create a quest map. ● Children's written responses and notes on their oral responses.	**Writing AF1** ● Mostly relevant ideas and content, sometimes repetitive or sparse. ● Some apt word choices create interest. ● Brief comments, questions about events or actions suggest viewpoint.	**Writing AF1** ● Some appropriate ideas and content included. ● Some attempt to elaborate on basic information or events. ● Attempt to adopt viewpoint, though often not maintained or inconsistent.	I can create a group quest map.
Telling the story Children can tell a story orally, organised in a clear sequence.	● Independent activity where children retell a chosen quest myth. ● Notes on children's oral responses.	**Writing AF7** ● Simple, often speech-like vocabulary conveys relevant meanings. ● Some adventurous word choices.	**Writing AF7** ● Simple, generally appropriate vocabulary used, limited in range. ● Some words selected for effect or occasion.	I can retell a quest story orally.

Unit 2 📖 Myths and legends

Learning outcomes	Assessment opportunity and evidence	Assessment focuses (AFs)		Success criteria
		Level 2	Level 3	
Phase ③ activities pages 41–43				
Write an opening Children can write a complete quest myth organised into a clear sequence of events.	• Supported group activity where children write a story opening. • Peer-assessment. • Children's written responses and notes made on their oral responses.	**Writing AF7** • Simple, often speech-like vocabulary conveys relevant meanings. • Some adventurous word choices.	**Writing AF7** • Simple, generally appropriate vocabulary used, limited in range. • Some words selected for effect or occasion.	I can write an opening for a quest story.
Character descriptions Children can write a complete quest myth organised into a clear sequence of events.	• Independent activity where children choose adjectives to describe characters. • Children's completed interactive activity, written responses and notes made on their oral responses.	**Writing AF7** • Simple, often speech-like vocabulary conveys relevant meanings. • Some adventurous word choices.	**Writing AF7** • Simple, generally appropriate vocabulary used, limited in range. • Some words selected for effect or occasion.	I can describe characters.
Endings Children can write a complete quest myth organised into a clear sequence of events.	• Supported group activity where children present and evaluate their quest myth ending. • Peer-assessment. • Children's written outcomes.	**Writing AF1** • Mostly relevant ideas and content, sometimes repetitive or sparse. • Some apt word choices create interest. • Brief comments, questions about events or actions suggest viewpoint.	**Writing AF1** • Some appropriate ideas and content included. • Some attempt to elaborate on basic information or events. • Attempt to adopt viewpoint, though often not maintained or inconsistent.	I can write an ending.

Learning outcomes	Assessment opportunity and evidence	Assessment focuses (AFs)		Success criteria
		Level 4	Level 5	
Phase ① activities pages 35–38				
Different genres Children can identify the main features of a quest myth.	• Independent activity where children match story titles to their genre. • Children's responses to the interactive activity and notes on their oral responses.	**Reading AF7** • Features common to different texts or versions of the same text identified, with simple comment. • Simple comment on the effect that the reader's or writer's context has on the meaning of texts.	**Reading AF7** • Comments identify similarities and differences between texts, or versions, with some explanation. • Some explanation of how the contexts in which texts are written and read contribute to meaning.	I can identify genres of stories.
Features of a quest myth Children can identify the main features of a quest myth.	• Independent activity where children discuss and identify features of a quest myth. • Children's written responses.	**Reading AF2** • Some relevant points identified. • Comments supported by some generally relevant textual reference or quotation.	**Reading AF2** • Most relevant points clearly identified, including those selected from different places in the text.	I can identify features of a quest myth.
Heroes and villains Children can identify the main features of a quest myth.	• Independent activity where children discuss and identify heroes and villains. • Notes made on children's oral responses and the completed interactive activity.	**Reading AF3** • Comments make inferences based on evidence from different points in the text. • Inferences often correct, but comments are not always rooted securely in the text or repeat narrative or content.	**Reading AF3** • Comments develop explanation of inferred meanings drawing on evidence across the text. • Comments make inferences and deductions based on textual evidence.	I can identify heroes and villains from myths.

Unit 2 ▢ Myths and legends

Learning outcomes	Assessment opportunity and evidence	Assessment focuses (AFs)		Success criteria
		Level 4	Level 5	
Create a character Children can identify the main features of a quest myth.	● Group activity where children create a hero, a villain for their quest story. ● Children's written responses.	**Writing AF7** ● Some evidence of deliberate vocabulary choices. ● Some expansion of general vocabulary to match topic.	**Writing AF7** ● Vocabulary chosen for effect. ● Reasonably wide vocabulary used, though not always appropriately.	I can plan elements for a quest story.

Phase ② activities pages 39–41

Learning outcomes	Assessment opportunity and evidence	Level 4	Level 5	Success criteria
Develop the setting ● Children can question others to find out further detail about a narrative. ● Children can tell a story orally, organised in a clear sequence.	● Paired activity where children generate ideas for a quest story. ● Peer-assessment. ● Notes made on children's oral responses.	**Writing AF3** ● Ideas organised by clustering related points or by time sequence. ● Ideas are organised simply with a fitting opening and closing, sometimes linked. ● Ideas or material generally in logical sequence but overall direction of writing not always clearly signalled.	**Writing AF3** ● Material is structured clearly, with sentences organised into appropriate paragraphs. ● Development of material is effectively managed across text. ● Overall direction of the text supported by clear links between paragraphs.	● I can discuss ideas with a partner, and describe our ideas to others. ● I can question others to find out about their ideas.
Group maps ● Children can question others to find out further detail about a narrative. ● Children can tell a story orally, organised in a clear sequence.	● Independent group activity where children create a quest map. ● Children's written responses and notes on their oral responses.	**Writing AF1** ● Relevant ideas and content chosen. ● Some ideas and material developed in detail. ● Straightforward viewpoint generally established and maintained.	**Writing AF1** ● Relevant ideas and material developed with some imaginative detail. ● Development of ideas and material appropriately shaped for selected form. ● Clear viewpoint established, generally consistent, with some elaboration.	I can create a group quest map.
Telling the story Children can tell a story orally, organised in a clear sequence.	● Independent activity where children retell a chosen quest myth. ● Notes made on children's oral responses.	**Writing AF7** ● Some evidence of deliberate vocabulary choices. ● Some expansion of general vocabulary to match topic.	**Writing AF7** ● Vocabulary chosen for effect. ● Reasonably wide vocabulary used, though not always appropriately.	I can retell a quest story orally.

Phase ③ activities pages 41–43

Learning outcomes	Assessment opportunity and evidence	Level 4	Level 5	Success criteria
Write an opening Children can write a complete quest myth organised into a clear sequence of events.	● Independent activity where children write a story opening. ● Peer-assessment. ● Children's written responses.	**Writing AF7** ● Some evidence of deliberate vocabulary choices. ● Some expansion of general vocabulary to match topic.	**Writing AF7** ● Vocabulary chosen for effect. ● Reasonably wide vocabulary used, though not always appropriately.	I can write an opening for a quest story.
Character descriptions Children can write a complete quest myth organised into a clear sequence of events	● Independent activity where children choose adjectives to describe characters. ● Children's completed interactive activity, and written responses.	**Writing AF7** ● Some evidence of deliberate vocabulary choices. ● Some expansion of general vocabulary to match topic.	**Writing AF7** ● Vocabulary chosen for effect. ● Reasonably wide vocabulary used, though not always appropriately.	I can describe characters.
Endings Children can write a complete quest myth organised into a clear sequence of events.	● Unsupported group activity where children present and evaluate their quest myth ending. ● Children's written outcomes and peer-assessment.	**Writing AF1** ● Relevant ideas and content chosen. ● Some ideas and material developed in detail. ● Straightforward viewpoint generally established and maintained.	**Writing AF1** ● Relevant ideas and material developed with some imaginative detail. ● Development of ideas and material appropriately shaped for selected form. ● Clear viewpoint established, generally consistent.	I can write an ending.

Phase ① Different genres

Learning outcome
Children can identify the main features of a quest myth.

Success criteria
I can identify genres of stories.

Setting the context
This activity should be carried out once the children have been introduced to several examples of stories in a variety of genres (myth, legend, fairy tale, traditional tale and fable) and have compared them with the common elements of quest stories, for example, *Mulan* or *The Hobbit.* Provide the children with the photocopiable page 'Different genres'. Read the story titles together and ensure they are familiar with the stories. If necessary, give a brief summary of any stories that are new to them. They should cut out the cards and group the story titles according to the genre. Alternatively, they can work on the interactive activity 'Different genres' to categorise the titles by genre.

Assessment opportunity
Children working at levels 2-3 work in a supported discussion group. An adult can ask questions to draw out the children's responses, for example: *What happens in 'Cinderella' that makes you match it to 'fairy tale'? Why don't you think 'The Three Little Pigs' is a legend? Can you tell me what happens in the story 'The Lion and the Mouse'? Why do you think it is a fable?* (It has a moral.) *What lesson or moral do we learn from the story?* Children working at levels 4-5 will work independently. Ask them to discuss their answers and to give reasons why they put the titles into specific genres.

Assessment evidence
At levels 2-3, children will recognise the general features of some of the different text types. At levels 4-5, children will identify more clearly the similarities and differences between different genres and will have some understanding of the context in which each text type may have been written. Use notes on the children's discussions as evidence towards Reading AF7.

Next steps
Support: Provide label cards (myth, legend, fairy tale, traditional tale, fable) and a selection of stories. Add typical features to the labels, for example: fairy tale – magic; fable – animal characters. Ask children to group the stories with the correct label.
Extension: Ask children to choose one story to read from each genre.

Key aspects of learning
Social skills: When working collaboratively, children will listen to and respect other people's ideas.
Communication: Children will develop their ability to discuss as they work collaboratively in paired, group and whole-class contexts. They will communicate outcomes orally, in writing and through ICT if appropriate.

NARRATIVE

Phase ① Features of a quest myth

Learning outcome
Children can identify the main features of a quest myth.

Success criteria
I can identify features of a quest myth.

Setting the context
This activity should be undertaken after the children have read and analysed a quest myth. Remind them that quest myths usually feature a hero, a monster, a dangerous or difficult journey, a mysterious helper, a magical tool or weapon, and problems that the hero meets. Provide the children with copies of photocopiable page 'Features of a quest myth' (versions 1 and 2). Ask children working at levels 2–3 to identify the features from the box at the bottom of the page by highlighting them or underlining them in different colours. Children working at levels 4–5 could use version 2 of the photocopiable page, which does not list the features to be found.

Assessment opportunity
Children working at levels 2–3 work in a supported group. An adult can read the quest myth aloud to the group and ask questions to prompt them to think about the features of the story, for example: *Who is the king's bravest knight? What does the king want the knight to do and why? What will happen if the knight fails? What problems does the knight meet? Who helps the knight to solve the problems? Why does the eagle give the knight a silver dagger?* A supporting adult can make notes of the children's responses. Children can then complete the photocopiable page independently after discussion. Children working at levels 4–5 can complete the photocopiable page independently.

Assessment evidence
At levels 2–3 children will show that, with support, they can retrieve from a text the information that they need to determine its key features. At levels 4–5, children will retrieve this information independently and from a variety of different places in the text. Use the completed photocopiable pages and the notes made on the children's responses to provide evidence for Reading AF2.

Next steps
Support: For those who struggled to find the features in the text, send a similar list of questions home with other myths and quest stories for further practice in recognising the typical features.
Extension: After personal reading of myths, ask the children to summarise the features for the rest of the class and compare the similarities and differences in different stories.

Key aspects of learning
Empathy: Writing and listening to stories will help children to understand what others might be thinking or feeling in a particular situation.
Social skills: When working collaboratively, children will listen to and respect other people's ideas.
Communication: Children will develop their ability to discuss as they work collaboratively in paired, group and whole-class contexts. They will communicate outcomes orally, in writing and through ICT if appropriate.

Phase ① Heroes and villains

Learning outcome
Children can identify the main features of a quest myth.

Success criteria
I can identify heroes and villains from myths.

Setting the context
This activity should be undertaken after the children have discussed the different kinds of character, both heroes and villains, who feature in typical myths. The photocopiable page 'Heroes and villains' and the 'Heroes and villains' interactive activity also feature pictures of heroes and villains. Read the names of the characters to the children and ask them if they have heard of them before. If they are unfamiliar with any of them, briefly summarise their role and the story in which they feature without using the terms 'hero' or 'villain'. Children match the pictures with text to identify which could be heroes and which villains. Both activities replicate each other in different forms to suit different learning styles, although the photocopiable page is slightly more challenging as children need to identify both the names of the characters and whether they are heroes or villains. On the interactive activity the characters are named for the children. Invite the children to state which hero and which villain they prefer and why.

Assessment opportunity
Children working at levels 2-3 can work in a supported group and discuss who the characters on the photocopiable page are before deciding if they are heroes or villains. Alternatively, the interactive activity can be undertaken independently. Children working at levels 4-5 identify the types of character independently, either on the photocopiable page or on the interactive activity. The children's preferences and reasons for them can be noted.

Assessment evidence
At levels 2-3, children will classify a character using straightforward inference that is based on a single point of reference or a literal interpretation. At levels 4-5, children will base their classification on a wider range of evidence, inferences and deductions. Use the children's written responses and the completed interactive activity to provide evidence for Reading AF3.

Next steps
Support: Create character cards of a range of heroes and villains from different stories and invite children to sort them into the two categories.
Extension: The children draw and name their own characters for quest myths.

Key aspects of learning
Social skills: When working collaboratively, children will listen to and respect other people's ideas.
Communication: Children will develop their ability to discuss as they work collaboratively in paired, group and whole-class contexts. They will communicate outcomes orally, in writing and through ICT if appropriate.

NARRATIVE

Phase ① Create a character

Learning outcome
Children can identify the main features of a quest myth.

Success criteria
I can plan elements for a quest story.

Setting the context
This activity should be undertaken after the children have explored and discussed the appearance and characteristics of heroes and villains that feature in quest myths. They should also have explored the magical elements that occur in myths such as a helper or a magical tool. Invite the children to work in small groups to create a hero and a villain for a new quest myth, and to decide what magical element they would like to include. When they have reached a joint decision, ask them to draw the hero, villain and magical element and label them with details about their characteristics.

Assessment opportunity
Children working at levels 2-3 work in a supported group. An adult working with the group can ask questions to draw out and deepen their responses and make notes of them on the class list. Example questions could be: *Do you want your hero to be especially strong or fast? Do you think he or she ought to have a weakness? What will he or she need to help overcome the weakness? Why does your hero need to defeat the villain? Has the villain got any weaknesses that the hero can use to beat him? How do you want your hero/villain to look? How can you describe your hero's personality when you label the picture?* (For example, brave.) *Can you think of any other words that have a similar meaning?* (For example, fearless.) Children working at levels 4-5 report the outcome of their group decision.

Assessment evidence
At levels 2-3, children will use simple and effective vocabulary that is generally appropriate and may feature the occasional more adventurous word. Children working at levels 4-5 will draw upon a wider range of vocabulary, deliberately choosing more words for their particular effects. Use the children's annotated drawings and the notes on their oral responses as evidence towards Writing AF7.

Next steps
Support: For those who struggled to choose interesting vocabulary to label their pictures, encourage the use of a thesaurus to improve the wording of the labels.
Extension: Children write a character sketch for their hero and their villain.

Key aspects of learning
Social skills: When working collaboratively, children will listen to and respect other people's ideas.
Communication: Children will develop their ability to discuss as they work collaboratively in paired, group and whole-class contexts. They will communicate outcomes orally, in writing and through ICT if appropriate.

Phase ② Develop the setting

Learning outcomes
- Children can question others to find out further detail about a narrative.
- Children can tell a story orally, organised in a clear sequence.

Success criteria
- I can discuss ideas with a partner, and describe our ideas to others.
- I can question others to find out about their ideas.

Setting the context
This activity should be undertaken after the children have had opportunities to read and analyse a number of myths in shared, guided and personal reading. They should have discussed the settings and perils encountered on the journey by the heroes of the stories. The children work with a partner and explore the story map for a quest myth using photocopiable page 'Develop the setting'. Invite the pairs to discuss the journey a hero would need to make on the map and the perils he or she would face and overcome to reach the end of the journey. They should make brief notes as they work out the journey and events.

Assessment opportunity
Children working at levels 2–3 work in pairs with a supporting adult to discuss details of the journey. An adult working with the supported pair can make notes of their ideas on the class list. Pairs of children then describe the journey to a different pair. They evaluate each other's journey ideas, questioning and commenting on them. Encourage the children to find two ideas each that they think would make exciting events in a quest myth. Children working at levels 4–5 work in pairs to plan the hero's journey through the places featured on the map and make notes of the perils the hero meets.

Assessment evidence
At levels 2–3, children will try to organise their ideas and to sequence logically the stages of the hero's journey. Children working at levels 4–5 will make links between different parts of the journey. They will pay more attention to the opening and closing of the story and will make clear to the reader in more detail the time span within which the events occur. Use the children's writing and the notes on their oral responses, made on the class list, as evidence towards Writing AF3.

Next steps:
Support: Encourage children to borrow events from myths they have read when they struggle to think of new events for the places on the map.
Extension: Write a setting description based on the map.

Key aspects of learning:
Reasoning: Children will predict and anticipate events in their own quest myth, based on the actions of key characters and settings using the language of cause and effect.
Social skills: When working collaboratively, children will listen to and respect other people's ideas.
Communication: Children will develop their ability to discuss as they work collaboratively in paired, group and whole-class contexts. They will communicate outcomes orally, in writing and through ICT if appropriate.

NARRATIVE

Phase ② Group maps

Learning outcomes
- Children can question others to find out further detail about a narrative.
- Children can tell a story orally, organised in a clear sequence.

Success criteria
I can create a group quest map.

Setting the context
This activity should be undertaken when children have analysed different quest myths and explored story maps. The children work in small groups to create a quest map. They will make suggestions about the journey the map will show and listen and respond to each other's ideas. Invite them to discuss what happens in their quest, and what features of landscape they will include to challenge their hero. Ask them to draw and label the features of the journey on the map.

Assessment opportunity
Children working at levels 2-3 work in a supported group. An adult can ask questions to draw out and deepen their responses and to ensure that each group member makes a contribution to the discussion and has the opportunity to contribute to the drawing and labelling of their map. Children working at levels 4-5 work in an independent group.

Assessment evidence
At levels 2-3, children will generate relevant ideas, though these may be repetitive or sparse. Children working at levels 4-5 will include more imaginative detail, marking on their maps some unusual or surprising features and extending and developing some of their ideas to form a consistent thread running right through the journey. Use the annotated maps and notes to provide evidence for Writing AF1.

Next steps
Support: Encourage those who struggled to add to their group story map, to create individual story maps for stories they have read and enjoyed in other genres.
Extension: Children write a setting description based on their story map.

Key aspects of learning
Reasoning: Children will predict and anticipate events in their own quest myth based on the actions of key characters and settings, using the language of cause and effect.
Empathy: Writing and listening to stories will help children to understand what others might be thinking or feeling in a particular situation.
Social skills: When working collaboratively, children will listen to and respect other people's ideas.
Communication: Children will develop their ability to discuss as they work collaboratively in paired, group and whole-class contexts. They will communicate outcomes orally, in writing and through ICT if appropriate.

Phase ② Telling the story

Learning outcome
Children can tell a story orally, organised in a clear sequence.

Success criteria
I can retell a quest story orally.

Setting the context
This activity should be undertaken after the children have become familiar with several quest myths and the features of the genre. Invite the children to choose one of the quest myths. Ask them one at a time, over several days, to retell the story to you orally in their own words. Encourage them to use a variety of connective words and phrases to sequence their retelling rather than repeating 'and then...'.

◼SCHOLASTIC

Assessment opportunity
Make notes as the children retell the story, focusing on their vocabulary choices and the amount of interesting detail they include. Children working at levels 2-3 may refer to the book to help them recall the sequence of events. Those children who are unable to choose a myth can use the *Beowulf* prompts on the photocopiable page 'Telling the story' as an aid to retelling the story. Those who need practice in sequencing events can use the interactive activity 'Telling the story'.

Assessment evidence
At levels 2-3, children will use simple language, often resembling direct speech. They will employ mundane but appropriate vocabulary peppered with the occasional more exciting word. Children working at levels 4-5 will deliberately choose words for their effect and will be more successful in employing a range of connective words and phrases to sequence their retelling. Use the notes made as you listened to the children's storytelling to provide evidence towards Writing AF7.

Next steps
Support: Provide prompts - opening, the task, the journey, the ending - to help children retell events in the correct order. Collect lists of connecting words and phrases to use in storytelling and write them in their reading journals.
Extension: Invite children to retell their chosen quest myth orally to the class.

Key aspects of learning
Social skills: When working collaboratively, children will listen to and respect other people's ideas.
Communication: Children will develop their ability to discuss as they work collaboratively in paired, group and whole-class contexts. They will communicate outcomes orally, in writing and through ICT if appropriate.

Phase ③ Write an opening

Learning outcome
Children can write a complete quest myth organised into a clear sequence of events.

Success criteria
I can write an opening for a quest story.

Setting the context
This activity should be undertaken after the children have explored characters, settings and plots in quest myths. They should have made decisions about heroes and villains and created quest-myth maps. They should also have experienced writing sessions that focus on different ways of creating story openings. Provide the children with the photocopiable page 'Write an opening' (versions 1 or 2) and ask them to write notes of descriptive words and phrases to describe the hero, the setting and the villain of the story. They then write a short paragraph to open their quest myth. Suggest that they introduce the setting and either the hero or the villain, but not both at once. Children working at levels 4-5 can use version 2 of the photocopiable page to write a couple of paragraphs of their myth.

Assessment opportunity
Children working at levels 2-3 work in a supported group, each with a copy of the photocopiable page 'Write an opening' (version 1). An adult can ask questions to help them organise their ideas, for example: *Which character are you going to introduce first, your hero or the villain? 'Once upon a time' is often used in fairy tales. Can you think of a different way to begin your first sentence?* (For example, X was a cruel monster'.) *That is really good... can you think of how to add some description of the story setting to that sentence?* (For example, X was a cruel monster who lived in...') Children working at levels 4-5 work independently to write notes on version 2 of the photocopiable page and write their opening paragraph. Ask the children to swap their completed pages with a partner to carry out a

peer-assessment. The children evaluate each other's story openings and make a note of two good things and one that could be improved.

Assessment evidence
At levels 2-3, children will use simple, everyday vocabulary and the occasional more interesting word. At levels 4-5, children will deliberately choose words for their effect, showing a wider range of vocabulary choices. Use your notes and the children's written responses to provide evidence for Writing AF7.

Next steps
Support: Provide a list of connectives to help them sequence their story opening, for example: 'later', 'although', 'despite' and so on.
Extension: Children write a second paragraph to extend their story opening.

Key aspects of learning
Reasoning: Children will predict and anticipate events in their own quest myth based on the actions of key characters and settings, using the language of cause and effect.
Evaluation: Children will discuss criteria for their written work, give feedback to others and judge the effectiveness of their own descriptions.
Empathy: Writing and listening to stories will help children to understand what others might be thinking or feeling in a particular situation.
Social skills: When working collaboratively, children will listen to and respect other people's ideas.
Communication: Children will develop their ability to discuss as they work collaboratively in paired, group and whole-class contexts. They will communicate outcomes orally, in writing and through ICT if appropriate.

Phase ③ Character descriptions

Learning outcome
Children can write a complete quest myth organised into a clear sequence of events.

Success criteria
I can describe characters.

Setting the context
This activity should be undertaken when the children have had experience of creating character sketches. Ensure the children have explored the use of adjectives to improve their writing. Children use the interactive activity 'Character descriptions' and drag and drop powerful adjectives to commonly-used adjectives to describe characters from a quest myth. After each choice has been made, invite the children to say which adjective they would prefer to use, how they would use it and why.

Assessment opportunity
Children working at levels 2-3 can use a thesaurus to help them choose the correct adjectives. Children working at levels 4-5 can independently select the adjectives that are the most similar in meaning. Make notes of children's comments. Invite the children to write their own character description of either a hero, a villain or a monster using the alternative adjectives from the interactive activity.

Assessment evidence
At levels 2-3, children will generally choose simple vocabulary - given this opportunity to find new words they may remain conservative in their choices or branch out to use the occasional new one. At levels 4-5, children will deliberately choose their vocabulary for maximum effect. Use the completed interactive activities, written responses and your notes to provide evidence for Writing AF7.

Next steps
Support: Encourage children to use any of the adjectives they are unfamiliar with in a sentence orally and to add them to their reading journals or personal dictionaries.

Extension: Children write the pairs of adjectives in a list and add a third adjective to each pair, then write them in a sentence.

Key aspects of learning
Communication: Children will develop their ability to discuss as they work collaboratively in paired, group and whole-class contexts. They will communicate outcomes orally, in writing and through ICT if appropriate.

Phase ③ Endings

Learning outcome
Children can write a complete quest myth organised into a clear sequence of events.

Success criteria
I can write an ending.

Setting the context
This activity should be undertaken after the children have worked in groups to create a quest-myth story map (see Phase 2 activity on page 40), written the opening of a quest myth and added a sequence of events. They should have had practice at writing the ending of quest myths and other stories. Invite the children to work in their groups with their quest-myth story maps. Ask each group to describe the story that takes place on their map, but omit the ending. Invite each member of the group to then write their own endings individually. When they finish, ask them to read their endings aloud to the group. Invite the group members to peer-assess: evaluate each other's endings and choose the ones they feel are the most successful. Ask them to support their choices of endings with reasons.

Assessment opportunity
The children working at levels 2–3 work with a supporting adult. Supporting adults can ask questions to enhance the children's responses, for example: *How does your hero feel at the end of the story? How do the other characters feel about the hero? Will they be changed in any way at the end of the story?* When evaluating each other's endings, a supporting adult can draw out the reasons for their opinions and make notes of each child's contribution. Children working at levels 4–5 work in unsupported groups. The children's notes on their evaluations of others' work will show whether they can identify the key features of a good ending.

Assessment evidence
At levels 2–3, children will include some appropriate ideas and content though their ideas may be repetitive or sparse. They will attempt to adopt an authorial voice and to elaborate but will find this difficult to maintain. At levels 4–5, children will establish a more confident voice and will create more thoughtful and interesting endings. They will include more imaginative detail and the material will be fit for purpose. The children's written responses provide evidence for Writing AF1.

Next steps
Support: For those who struggled to write an ending, select some of the best story endings to use as models on which they can base their own story endings.
Extension: Encourage children to write their quest myth in full.

Key aspects of learning
Reasoning: Children will predict and anticipate events in their own quest myth based on the actions of key characters and settings, using the language of cause and effect.
Evaluation: Children will discuss criteria for their written work, give feedback to others and judge the effectiveness of their own descriptions.
Social skills: When working collaboratively, children will listen to and respect other people's ideas.

NARRATIVE

Periodic assessment

Reading

Learning outcome
Children can identify the main features of a quest myth, including the introduction of the main characters, the problem to be overcome, the journey undertaken and the resolution to the problem.

Success criteria
- I can identify features of a quest myth.
- I can select and describe information from a quest myth.

Setting the context
This activity should be carried out once the children have completed Narrative Unit 2. Children read a quest myth, 'The story of Kuang-li' on photocopiable page 'Narrative 2 Reading assessment text', and are given a copy of 'Narrative 2 Reading assessment', and asked to answer nine questions about the story. The question types range from literal, about the subject, and evaluative, about the type of hero. Read the extract aloud to the children before providing them with their own copy, or display it on screen. Identify any new, unusual or difficult vocabulary for the children before giving them their copy in order to pre-empt any problems in their understanding of the passage. Ask them to re-read the text carefully. Tell them to annotate or note any quest-myth features that strike them before reading the questions. Explain that doing this will help them to answer the questions as well as they can.

Assessment opportunity
The children should be given sufficient time in which to read and digest the description and to annotate it before answering the questions. This activity provides an opportunity to assess the children's ability to recognise the typical features and the overall effectiveness of the quest myth.

Assessment evidence
The children's annotated texts and written responses will provide evidence for Reading AF2, AF3, AF5 and AF6. Children working at levels 2–3 will respond to the text at a literal level, making simple inferences based on single points of reference. They will successfully recall information or know where to find it and will note but not comment on the author's use of language. Children working at levels 4–5 will make inferences and deductions from the text – and this will help them to answer questions 7, 8 and 9. Use this activity as well as examples of children's work throughout this unit to make a level judgement for Reading.

Periodic assessment

Writing

Learning outcome
Children can write a complete quest myth organised into a clear sequence of events.

Success criteria
I can create a plan for writing a quest myth.

Setting the context
This should be carried out once the children have completed Narrative Unit 2. Children are given a copy of the writing frame and prompts on the photocopiable page 'Narrative 2 Writing assessment'. Remind them about the work they have completed during the unit, and about the typical features of a quest myth. Explain that they are to make notes of ideas for writing a complete quest myth that include all the features they have explored in the course of this unit. Invite them to make brief notes of words and phrases and ideas for the story rather than writing in complete sentences. Remind them that their notes need to be legible.

Assessment opportunity
This activity provides an opportunity to assess the children's understanding of the work they have completed in the course of the unit and their ability to put it into practice to create an effective plan for a myth that includes the features they have been exploring. It also provides the opportunity to assess each child's ability to plan a whole story with a beginning, middle and ending, and a clearly structured sequence of events. Children working at levels 2–3 work with a supporting adult to draw out and clarify their ideas, for example, asking: *What sort of hero do you want? What makes your hero special? What does the hero need to overcome the problem? How long do you think the journey will take? What is the landscape like?* (For example, rocky and tough.) *Why not make a note of those words on the plan?* The supporting adult can make notes of each child's comments and ideas on the class list to provide evidence to complement their completed plans.

Assessment evidence
The children's written responses to the notes made on the class list will provide evidence for Writing AF1 and AF3. Children working at levels 2–3 will include some appropriate ideas and content, though these may be repetitive or sparse. Their plan will be in a logical sequence. Simple language will be used to describe events, with only the occasional word chosen for effect. Children working at levels 4–5 will produce more imaginative and thoughtful plans. They will show in more detail how the plot develops, with clear links between each stage and echoes between stages, making a cohesive whole. Use this activity as well as examples of children's work throughout this unit to make a level judgement for Writing.

Name _____ Date _____

Heroes and villains

■ Write the name under each character and add either 'hero' or 'villain'.

_____

_____

_____

_____

_____

_____

_____

_____

_____

_____

_____

_____

| Beowulf | Minotaur | Medusa | Mulan | Grendel | Perseus |

Illustrations © 2009, Anna Godwin.

Red
Amber
Green

I can identify heroes and villains from myths. ☐

Develop the setting

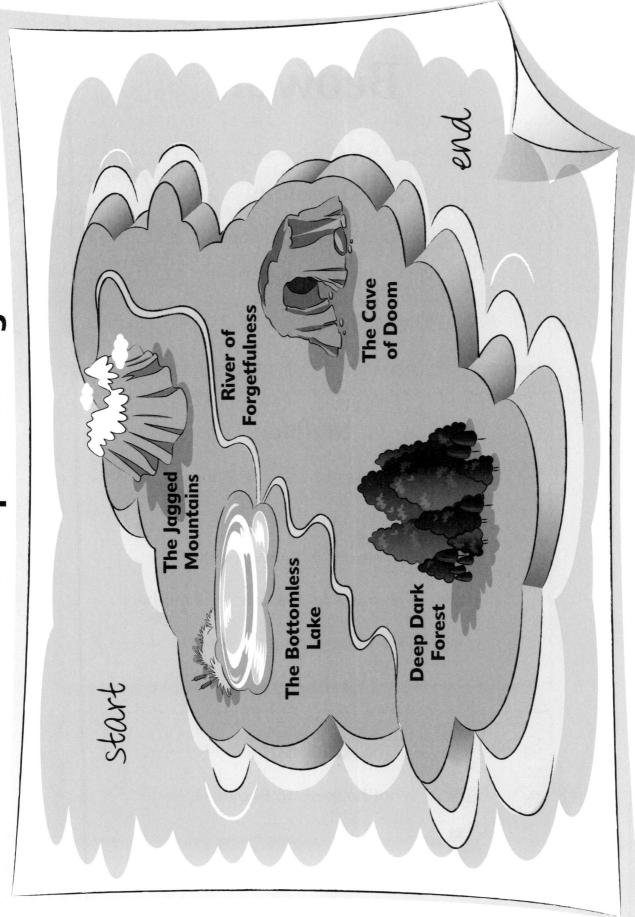

start

The Jagged
Mountains

River of
Forgetfulness

The Bottomless
Lake

The Cave
of Doom

Deep Dark
Forest

end

NARRATIVE

Telling the story

Beowulf

Opening:

What is the story about?

Who is Grendel?

Why do the Danes need a hero?

Middle:

Who comes to help the Danes?

Who does Beowulf fight first?

Who else does Beowulf fight?

Why does Beowulf follow Grendel's mother?

How does Beowulf slay the monsters?

Ending:

What happens to Beowulf?

Illustrations © 2009, Anna Godwin.

Name   Date

Write an opening (1)

◼ Draw and make notes about the hero, setting and villain of your story.

Hero	Setting	Villain

◼ Now write a short paragraph to open your story.

Red   Amber   Green 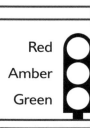   I can write an opening for a quest story. ☐

NARRATIVE
UNIT 3 Adventure and mystery

Literacy objectives

Speak and listen for a wide range of purposes in different contexts
Strand 3 Group discussion and interaction
- Use the language of possibility to investigate and reflect on feelings, behaviour or relationships.

Strand 4 Drama
- Use some drama strategies to explore stories or issues.

Read and write or a range of purposes on paper and on screen
Strand 7 Understanding and interpreting texts
- Infer characters' feelings in fiction and consequences in logical explanations.
- Explore how different texts appeal to readers using varied sentence structures and descriptive language.

Strand 8 Engaging with and responding to texts
- Share and compare reasons for reading preferences, extending the range of books read.
- Empathise with characters and debate moral dilemmas portrayed in texts.
- Identify features that writers use to provoke readers' reactions.

Strand 9 Creating and shaping texts
- Make decisions about form and purpose, identify success criteria and use them to evaluate their writing.
- Use beginning, middle and end to write narratives in which events are sequenced logically and conflicts resolved.
- Select and use a range of technical and descriptive vocabulary.

Strand 10 Text structure and organisation
- Signal sequence, place and time to give coherence.
- Group related material into paragraphs.

Strand 11 Sentence structure and punctuation
- Show relationships of time, reason and cause through subordination and connectives.
- Compose sentences using adjectives, verbs and nouns for precision, clarity and impact.
- Clarify meaning through the use of exclamation marks and speech marks.

Key aspects of learning

Empathy
- By taking part in role-play activities, children will be able to identify with fictional characters and will be helped to understand their feelings and actions.

Creative thinking
- Children will use creative thinking to extend and consider alternatives to typical elements of an adventure story and create a new story of their own.

Communication
- Children will develop their ability to discuss aspects as they work collaboratively in paired, group and whole-class contexts. They will communicate outcomes orally, in writing and through ICT if appropriate.

Assessment focuses

Reading
AF2 *(understand, describe, select or retrieve information, events or ideas from texts and use quotation and reference to text).*
AF6 *(identify and comment on writers' purposes and viewpoints, and the overall effect of the text on the reader).*

Writing
AF1 *(write imaginative, interesting and thoughtful texts).*
AF2 *(produce texts which are appropriate to task, reader and purpose).*
AF3 *(organise and present whole texts effectively, sequencing and structuring information, ideas and events).*
AF5 *(vary sentences for clarity, purpose and effect).*
AF6 *(write with technical accuracy of syntax and punctuation in phrases, clauses and sentences).*
AF7 *(select appropriate and effective vocabulary).*

Speaking and listening
Group discussion and interaction (support others, take turns).
Drama (improvise and sustain roles).

Resources

Phase 1
Photocopiable page, 'Typical characters' (versions 1 and 2)
Photocopiable page, 'Planning a character'
Phase 2
Photocopiable page, 'Connecting words and phrases'
Interactive activity, 'Connecting words and phrases'
Interactive activity, 'Present- and past-tense verbs'
Photocopiable page, 'Write a letter'
Phase 3
Photocopiable page, 'Planning an adventure'
Periodic assessment
Photocopiable page, 'Narrative 3 Reading assessment'
Recommended texts
The Julian Stories by Ann Cameron (ISBN 978-0552-54824-3)
Julian, Secret Agent by Ann Cameron (ISBN 978-0394-81949-5)
Hostage by Malorie Blackman (ISBN 978-1842-99375-0)
Midnight for Charlie Bone by Jenny Nimmo (ISBN 978-1405-22543-4)
Red Eyes at Night by Michael Morpurgo (ISBN 978-0340-68753-6)
It's Too Frightening for Me by Shirley Hughes (ISBN 978-0140-32008-4)

Unit 3 ▣ Adventure and mystery

Learning outcomes	Assessment opportunity and evidence	Assessment focuses (AFs)		Success criteria
		Level 2	Level 3	
Phase ① activities pages 55-56				
Typical characters ● Children can identify key features of adventure stories. ● Children can explain reasons why a character has behaved in a particular way.	● Supported group activity where children discuss features of an adventure-story character. ● Children's written responses and notes made on their oral responses.	**Reading AF2** ● Some specific, straightforward information recalled. ● Generally clear idea of where to look for information.	**Reading AF2** ● Simple, most obvious points identified though there may also be some misunderstanding. ● Some comments include quotations from or references to text, but not always relevant.	I can identify features of an adventure-story character.
Planning a character ● Children can identify key features of adventure stories. ● Children can explain reasons why a character has behaved in a particular way.	● Supported paired activity where children plan a character for an adventure story. ● Children's written responses and notes made on their oral responses.	**Writing AF1** ● Mostly relevant ideas and content, sometimes repetitive or sparse. ● Some apt word choices create interest. ● Brief comments, questions about events or actions suggest viewpoint.	**Writing AF1** ● Some appropriate ideas and content included. ● Some attempt to elaborate on basic information or events. ● Attempt to adopt viewpoint, though often not maintained or inconsistent.	I can plan a character for an adventure story.
Phase ② activities pages 57-59				
Connecting words and phrases Children can recount an incident from a story maintaining a first-person viewpoint.	● Independent activity where children recount an event using the first person. ● Children's written responses and notes made on their oral responses.	**Writing AF7** ● Simple, often speech-like vocabulary conveys relevant meanings. ● Some adventurous word choices.	**Writing AF7** ● Simple, generally appropriate vocabulary used, limited in range. ● Some words selected for effect or occasion.	● I can describe an event using the first person. ● I can use connectives to link paragraphs in a first-person recount.
Present- and past-tense verbs Children can recount an incident from a story maintaining a first-person viewpoint.	● Supported activity where children practise using past- and present-tense verbs. ● Children's responses to the interactive activity and notes made on their oral responses.	**Writing AF5** ● Some variation in sentence openings. ● Mainly simple sentences with *and* used to connect clauses. ● Past and present tense generally consistent.	**Writing AF5** ● Reliance mainly on simply structured sentences, variation with support. ● *and, but, so* are the most common connectives, subordination occasionally. ● Some limited variation in use of tense and verb forms, not always secure.	I can use present- and past-tense verbs.
Write a letter Children can recount an incident from a story maintaining a first-person viewpoint.	● Supported group activity where children discuss ideas for a letter to a friend. ● Children's written responses and notes made on their oral responses.	**Writing AF2** ● Some basic purpose established. ● Some appropriate features of the given form used. ● Some attempts to adopt appropriate style.	**Writing AF2** ● Purpose established at a general level. ● Main features of selected form sometimes signalled to the reader. ● Some attempts at appropriate style, with attention to reader.	I can describe an event using the first person.
Phase ③ activities pages 59-60				
Planning an adventure Children can plan an extended narrative using the key features of the text type.	● Supported group activity where children write a story plan. ● Children's written responses and notes made on their oral responses.	**Writing AF3** ● Some basic sequencing of ideas or material. ● Openings and/or closings sometimes signalled.	**Writing AF3** ● Some attempt to organise ideas with related points placed next to each other. ● Openings and closings usually signalled. ● Some attempt to sequence ideas or material logically.	● I can plan characters and settings. ● I can plan a story outline.

Unit 3 ◻ Adventure and mystery

Learning outcomes	Assessment opportunity and evidence	Assessment focuses (AFs)		Success criteria
		Level 2	Level 3	
Dialogue Children can write an extended adventure story with logically sequenced events and resolution.	• Supported paired activity where children discuss dialogue. • Children's written responses and notes made on their oral responses.	**Writing AF6** • Clause structure mostly grammatically correct. • Sentence demarcation with capital letters and full stops usually accurate. • Some accurate use of question and exclamation marks, and commas in lists. **Writing AF7** • Simple, often speech-like vocabulary conveys relevant meanings. • Some adventurous word choices.	**Writing AF6** • Straightforward sentences usually demarcated accurately with full stops, capital letters, question and exclamation marks. • Some, limited, use of speech punctuation. • Comma splicing evident, particularly in narrative. **Writing AF7** • Simple, generally appropriate vocabulary used, limited in range. • Some words selected for effect or occasion.	• I can use dialogue in a story. • I can make a story exciting. • I can write a story ending.

Learning outcomes	Assessment opportunity and evidence	Assessment focuses (AFs)		Success criteria
		Level 4	Level 5	
Phase ① activities pages 55–56				
Typical characters • Children can identify key features of adventure stories. • Children can explain reasons why a character has behaved in a particular way.	• Independent group activity where children discuss features of an adventure-story character. • Children's written responses and notes made on their oral responses.	**Reading AF2** • Some relevant points identified. • Comments supported by some generally relevant textual reference or quotation.	**Reading AF2** • Most relevant points clearly identified, including those selected from different places in the text. • Comments generally supported by relevant textual reference or quotation, even when points made are not always accurate.	I can identify features of an adventure-story character.
Planning a character • Children can identify key features of adventure stories. • Children can explain reasons why a character has behaved in a particular way.	• Paired activity where children plan a character for an adventure story. • Children's written responses and notes made on their oral responses.	**Writing AF1** • Relevant ideas and content chosen. • Some ideas and material developed in detail. • Straightforward viewpoint generally established and maintained.	**Writing AF1** • Relevant ideas and material developed with some imaginative detail. • Development of ideas and material appropriately shaped for selected form. • Clear viewpoint established, generally consistent, with some elaboration.	I can plan a character for an adventure story.
Phase ② activities pages 57–59				
Connecting words and phrases Children can recount an incident from a story maintaining a first-person viewpoint.	• Independent activity where children recount an event using the first person. • Children's written responses and notes made on their oral responses.	**Writing AF7** • Some evidence of deliberate vocabulary choices. • Some expansion of general vocabulary to match topic.	**Writing AF7** • Vocabulary chosen for effect. • Reasonably wide vocabulary used, though not always appropriately.	• I can describe an event using the first person. • I can use connectives to link paragraphs in a first-person recount.

Unit 3 ☐ Adventure and mystery

NARRATIVE

Learning outcomes	Assessment opportunity and evidence	Assessment focuses (AFs)		Success criteria
		Level 4	Level 5	
Present- and past-tense verbs Children can recount an incident from a story maintaining a first-person viewpoint.	● Independent activity where children practise using past- and present-tense verbs. ● Children's responses to the interactive activity and notes made on their oral responses.	**Writing AF5** ● Some variety in length, structure or subject of sentences. ● Use of some subordinating connectives throughout the text. ● Some variation, generally accurate, in tense and verb forms.	**Writing AF5** ● A variety of sentence lengths, structures and subjects provides clarity and emphasis. ● Wider range of connectives used to clarify relationship between ideas. ● Some features of sentence structure used to build up detail or convey shades of meaning.	I can use present- and past-tense verbs.
Write a letter Children can recount an incident from a story maintaining a first-person viewpoint.	● Independent activity where children write a letter to a friend. ● Children's written responses and notes made on their oral responses.	**Writing AF2** ● Main purpose of writing is clear but not always consistently maintained. ● Main features of selected form are clear and appropriate to purpose. ● Style generally appropriate to task, though awareness of reader not always sustained.	**Writing AF2** ● Main purpose of writing is clear and consistently maintained. ● Features of selected form clearly established with some adaptation to purpose. ● Appropriate style clearly established to maintain reader's interest throughout.	I can describe an event using the first person.

Phase ③ activities pages 59-60

Planning an adventure Children can plan an extended narrative using the key features of the text type.	● Paired activity where children write a story plan. ● Children's written responses and notes made on their oral responses.	**Writing AF3** ● Ideas organised by clustering related points or by time sequence. ● Ideas are organised simply with a fitting opening and closing, sometimes linked. ● Ideas or material generally in logical sequence but overall direction of writing not always clearly signalled.	**Writing AF3** ● Material is structured clearly, with sentences organised into appropriate paragraphs. ● Development of material is effectively managed across text. ● Overall direction of the text supported by clear links between paragraphs.	● I can plan characters and settings. ● I can plan a story outline.
Dialogue Children can write an extended adventure story with logically sequenced events and resolution.	● Paired activity where children write six short sentences of dialogue. ● Children's written responses and notes made on their oral responses.	**Writing AF6** ● Sentences demarcated accurately throughout the text, including question marks. ● Speech marks to denote speech generally accurate, with some other speech punctuation. ● Commas used in lists and occasionally to mark clauses, although not always accurate. **Writing AF7** ● Some evidence of deliberate vocabulary choices. ● Some expansion of general vocabulary to match topic.	**Writing AF6** ● Full range of punctuation used accurately to demarcate sentences, including speech punctuation. ● Syntax and punctuation within the sentence generally accurate including commas to mark clauses, though errors may occur where ambitious structures are attempted. **Writing AF7** ● Vocabulary chosen for effect. ● Reasonably wide vocabulary used, though not always appropriately.	● I can use dialogue in a story. ● I can make a story exciting. ● I can write a story ending.

■SCHOLASTIC

Phase ① Typical characters

Learning outcomes
● Children can identify key features of adventure stories.
● Children can explain reasons why a character has behaved in a particular way.

Success criteria
I can identify features of an adventure-story character.

Setting the context
This activity should be carried out once the children have read several adventure and mystery stories in shared, guided and independent reading. Examples of adventure stories to share with children include *The Julian Stories* and *Julian, Secret Agent* by Ann Cameron, *Hostage* by Malorie Blackman, *Midnight for Charlie Bone* by Jenny Nimmo and *Red Eyes at Night* by Michael Morpurgo. Ask the children to choose one of the stories they have recently read and enjoyed and select their favourite adventure-story character. Provide them with copies of photocopiable page 'Typical characters' (versions 1 or 2) and ask them to describe the character and why he or she appeals to them. Children working at levels 2–3 work in a discussion group supported by an adult, using version 1 of the photocopiable page. Those working at levels 4–5 work independently using version 2 of the photocopiable page.

Assessment opportunity
Children working at levels 2–3 work in a supported discussion group with an adult to draw out their responses by questioning, for example: *Does your character do anything unusual? Do any of the characters you have chosen in this group have anything in common? Are they all curious to find things out? Are any of them frightened or brave?* Ask the groups to share their pages and compare the results. Ask them to say which characteristics are the most common for adventure-story characters. Children working at levels 4–5 will work in small independent groups. They identify their favourite character, summarise his or her role in the story and select the best way to describe the character from a list of adjectives. They then write a sentence to explain their choice of character.

Assessment evidence
At levels 2–3, children will describe simply the most obvious and straightforward events affecting their chosen character. They will also choose adjectives that describe the character accurately. The events described by children working at levels 4–5 will draw more effectively on the story as a whole. These children may also explain why this particular character is their favourite. Use the children's notes and the findings they report orally – along with your notes made on their responses – to provide evidence for Reading AF2 (see also AF6).

Next steps
Support: For those who cannot identify common characteristics in adventure-story characters, create a character wall in the classroom and as the class meet characters in stories, add words to the character to describe him or her.
Extension: Ask the children to write a character sketch of their favourite character.

Key aspects of learning
Communication: Children will develop their ability to discuss as they work collaboratively in paired, group and whole-class contexts. They will communicate outcomes orally.

NARRATIVE

Phase ① Planning a character

Learning outcomes
● Children can identify key features of adventure stories.
● Children can explain reasons why a character has behaved in a particular way.

Success criteria
I can plan a character for an adventure story.

Setting the context
This activity should be undertaken after children have discussed and analysed several characters from a range of adventure stories. Discuss the character traits of some of the main characters that feature in stories the class has read. For example, in *Red Eyes at Night* by Michael Morpurgo, the main character, Millie, teases her cousin and in *The Julian Stories,* Julian teases his brother; in *It's Too Frightening for Me* by Shirley Hughes, Jim and Arthur are both frightened and curious; in *Midnight for Charlie Bone* by Jenny Nimmo, *Charlie Bone* is curious and brave. Ask them to think about how many characters in adventure stories they know who are orphans or outsiders, or have an unusual family and so on. Draw up a list of common features for the children to refer to. Ask the children to work with partners and provide them with copies of the photocopiable page 'Planning a character' and ask them to collaborate to create a new character for an adventure story.

Assessment opportunity
Children working at levels 2–3 work in pairs with a supporting adult to draw out their ideas by asking questions, for example: *How does your character's family contribute to the adventure? Why do you think his or her home might be important in the adventure? Is home a safe or a dangerous place? If he or she is frightened about something, why would they still want to find out about it?* A supporting adult can note comments on individual children's contributions. Children working at levels 4–5 complete the photocopiable page by collaborating with a partner.

Assessment evidence
At levels 2–3, children will come up with traits of character that are relevant and appropriate, though their ideas may be repetitive or sparse. In some cases they may try to elaborate with more information. At levels 4–5, children will develop their character in more detail, maintaining a consistent approach that is appropriate to the adventure story genre. Use the completed photocopiable pages as evidence towards Writing AF1.

Next steps
Support: Allow any who struggle to invent a character to fill in the photocopiable page using a character they have read about in an adventure story.
Extension: Children use their notes to role play their character and respond to questioning by other children.

Key aspects of learning
Empathy: By taking part in role-play activities, children will be able to identify with fictional characters and will be helped to understand their feelings and actions.
Creative thinking: Children will use creative thinking to extend and consider alternatives to typical elements of an adventure story.
Communication: Children will develop their ability to discuss as they work collaboratively in paired, group and whole-class contexts. They will communicate outcomes orally, in writing and through ICT if appropriate.

Phase ② Connecting words and phrases

Learning outcome
Children can recount an incident from a story maintaining a first-person viewpoint.

Success criteria
- I can describe an event using the first person.
- I can use connectives to link paragraphs in a first-person recount.

Setting the context
The children should have read about an incident in an adventure or mystery story. They should also have explored the use of connecting words and phrases to link paragraphs. Over a few days, children sit in the hotseat in the role of a character from an incident in a story and retell the incident using the first person. Encourage them to link the elements of their recount with connecting words and phrases other than 'and then...' and note comments. Provide children working at levels 2–3 with the photocopiable page 'Connecting words and phrases'. Children working at levels 4–5 work on the interactive activity 'Connecting words and phrases'.

Assessment opportunity
Children working at levels 2–3 complete the photocopiable page using the words in the box to help them. After they have completed the activity, ask the children to give reasons for their choices and make notes of individual responses. Children working at levels 4–5 complete the interactive assessment activity independently.

Assessment evidence
At levels 2–3, children will favour the more simple connectives 'and', 'but' and 'so' and may sometimes fail to select appropriate words and phrases. At levels 4–5, children will independently use a wider range of connectives. They are more likely to choose connectives that are fit for purpose and will make the text more readable. Use the completed activities and the children's oral responses to provide evidence for Writing AF7.

Next steps
Support: Create an informal 'splat board' or word wall for children to add connecting words and phrases that they find in their own reading.
Extension: Children write their retold incident in a paragraph using connecting words and phrases.

Key aspects of learning
Communication: Children will develop their ability to discuss as they work collaboratively in paired, group and whole-class contexts. They will communicate outcomes orally, in writing and through ICT if appropriate.

Phase ② Present- and past-tense verbs

Learning outcome
Children can recount an incident from a story maintaining a first-person viewpoint.

Success criteria
I can use present- and past-tense verbs.

Setting the context
This activity should be undertaken after the children have read a story narrated in the first person using the present tense, for example, *Red Eyes at Night* by Michael Morpurgo. They should have practised changing verb tenses from present to past and vice versa. Ask the children to describe an incident from the story. They should then explain their opinions about stories written in the first person using the present tense. They can use the interactive activity 'Present- and past-tense verbs'.

Assessment opportunity

Question the children to draw out their opinions, for example: *How would the story be different if told using the past tense? Does the present tense make the story feel more 'immediate'? Does the present tense make you feel more involved with the story? Why do you think that?* Make notes of the children's responses. Children working at levels 2–3 work with a supporting adult on the activity. Those working at levels 4–5 complete the interactive activity independently.

Assessment evidence

At levels 2–3, children will not always be secure in their use of tense and verb forms; nevertheless their mastery of the past and present tense should generally be consistent. At levels 4–5, children will generally be accurate in their use of tense and verb forms and will be accustomed to using a variety of tenses in their own writing. Use the children's written responses and notes made during the guided discussion to provide evidence towards Writing AF5.

Next steps

Support: Send home three verbs every day for children who struggled to change verb tenses, and ask them to write them in their present- and past-tense forms.
Extension: Encourage children to change a piece of their recent past-tense story-writing into the present tense and describe how the effect has changed.

Key aspects of learning

Communication: Children will develop their ability to discuss as they work collaboratively in paired, group and whole-class contexts. They will communicate outcomes orally, in writing and through ICT if appropriate.

Phase ② Write a letter

Learning outcome
Children can recount an incident from a story maintaining a first-person viewpoint.

Success criteria
I can describe an event using the first person.

Setting the context
The children should have read or listened to more than one adventure or mystery story. Ask them to choose one story that they have enjoyed reading and imagine that the adventure happened to them. Ask them first to recount the incident orally and then invite them to use the photocopiable page 'Write a letter' to write a letter to a friend and tell them about an incident in the story using first-person verbs.

Assessment opportunity
Children working at levels 2–3 work in a supported group and discuss their chosen incident and the details to include in a letter. An adult working with the supported group can ask questions to draw out and deepen their responses, for example: *If you were character X, what sort of language would you use in a letter? Would it be chatty and informal? How much detail do you think your friend would like to know? Are you remembering to use 'I' instead of 'she'?* The adult can make notes on specific evidence of particular children using the first person consistently in their oral recounts. Children working at levels 4–5 write their letter independently.

Assessment evidence
At levels 2–3, children will use an appropriate style that is fit for purpose. At levels 4–5, children will maintain more strongly a consistent authorial voice throughout the content of their letters. Use the children's written responses to provide evidence for Writing AF2.

Next steps
Support: Encourage children to imagine themselves in a situation from their chosen story, to role play the incident with a partner.

▷ **Extension:** Children write a letter in response to the first letter.

Key aspects of learning
Empathy: Children will be able to identify with fictional characters and will be helped to understand their feelings and actions.
Communication: Children will develop their ability to discuss as they work collaboratively in paired, group and whole-class contexts. They will communicate outcomes orally, in writing and through ICT if appropriate.

Phase ③ Planning an adventure

Learning outcome
Children can plan an extended narrative using the key features of the text type.

Success criteria
● I can plan characters and settings.
● I can plan a story outline.

Setting the context
The children should have explored characters, settings and problems or dilemmas that feature in adventure stories. They should also have experienced different ways to plan stories. Children working at levels 2–3 work in small groups to plan their adventure story with a supporting adult. Those at levels 4–5 should work in pairs to make brief notes for characters, setting and the plot. Provide the children with copies of the photocopiable page 'Planning an adventure' and invite them to collaborate to plan a new adventure story.

Assessment opportunity
Children working at levels 2–3 work in a supported group. An adult working with the supported group can ask questions to draw out their ideas, for example: *You want the adventure to take place in a school. What sort of school is it? Do the children live in the school or come every day? Who is the main baddie in the story? Is it a teacher or a visitor or one of the children?* The adult should make notes on individual children's contributions. Observe the children working at levels 4–5 and make notes on their contributions to the discussion.

Assessment evidence
At levels 2–3, children will attempt to organise their ideas effectively, with the story opening and ending and most of the sequencing being clear and logical. At levels 4–5, children will further shape the material, for example, by including themes that link different parts of the text or endings that echo beginnings. The development and direction of the plot are generally clear and well-managed. Use the children's written responses and observational notes to provide evidence for Writing AF3.

Next steps
Support: Use the planner to make notes on stories and alter one or two of the elements, for example, adding a new character or event.
Extension: Encourage children to rewrite their notes using a story map and draw the setting as the background.

Key aspects of learning
Creative thinking: Children will use creative thinking to extend and consider alternatives to typical elements of an adventure story and create a new story of their own.
Communication: Children will develop their ability to discuss as they work collaboratively in paired, group and whole-class contexts. They will communicate outcomes orally, in writing and through ICT if appropriate.

NARRATIVE

Phase ③ Dialogue

Learning outcome
Children can write an extended adventure story with logically sequenced events and resolution.

Success criteria
- I can use dialogue in a story.
- I can make a story exciting.
- I can write a story ending.

Setting the context
The children should have had opportunities to plan the characters, settings, plot, events and endings for new adventure stories. They should have read and written dialogue, including using the correct punctuation and different speech verbs. Invite the children to work in pairs and, using their adventure story plans, discuss what the characters might say to each other in the different events of the story, including what they would say at the end of the story. Ask them to think of how the dialogue can make the story feel exciting, for example, using exclamations and questions. Encourage them to say aloud their ideas for dialogue, using expressive voices. Invite them to write the dialogue using correct speech punctuation and speech verbs.

Assessment opportunity
Children working at levels 2-3 work in pairs in small, supported groups. An adult working with the supported group can ask questions to stimulate imagination, for example: *If they are frightened, how would they say that? If they need to be quiet in this part of the story, can you think of another verb to use instead of 'said'?* Children working at levels 4-5 work independently to write up to six short passages of dialogue with a partner.

Assessment evidence
At levels 2-3, children will select appropriate vocabulary – which will be limited in range, but enlivened by the occasional more interesting word. Their use of speech punctuation may be inaccurate, but more simple punctuation will mostly be correct. At levels 4-5, children will use a wider vocabulary, choosing words deliberately for effect. They will use a wide range of punctuation, only making errors when they attempt more complex sentences. Use the written responses of the children and the notes made during the group work as evidence towards Writing AF7 and AF6.

Next steps
Support: Ask children to use different speech verbs to collect examples from their personal reading.
Extension: Allow children to role play their passages of dialogue for the class.

Key aspects of learning
Creative thinking: Children will use creative thinking to extend and consider alternatives to typical elements of an adventure story and create a new story of their own.
Communication: Children will develop their ability to discuss as they work collaboratively in paired, group and whole-class contexts. They will communicate outcomes orally, in writing and through ICT if appropriate.

■SCHOLASTIC

Periodic assessment

Reading

Learning outcomes
● Children can identify key features of adventure stories.
● Children can identify how the author engages the reader and maintains interest.

Success criteria
● I can describe features of an adventure story.
● I can explore the language an author uses in an adventure story.

Setting the context
This activity should be carried out once the children have completed Narrative Unit 3. Collect the work that has been completed during the course of the unit and discuss individual children's achievements with them. Ask them to suggest what they found difficult about the work in the unit and what they found easy and compare their responses with the comments made on the class list. Provide the children with copies of photocopiable page 'Narrative 3 Reading assessment' and invite them to answer the questions.

Assessment opportunity
Use this periodic assessment to enable children to identify their strengths, weaknesses and personal preferences as readers of adventure stories.

Assessment evidence
Children's responses to this assessment, and their writing from elsewhere in Unit 3, can be used as evidence towards Reading AF2, AF3, AF5 and AF6. Allow children working at levels 2-3 to expand orally on their written answers - which will be based on straightforward inferences and literal information retrieved from single points in the text. They will answer question 9, but will be unable to explain their reasons (question 10). Children working at levels 4-5 will infer meaning from evidence across the whole text. They will identify key features of the author's technique (in question 8, for example) and their effects on readers - including themselves. Use this activity as well as examples of children's work throughout this unit to make level judgements for Reading.

NARRATIVE

Periodic assessment

Writing

Learning outcome
Children can write an extended adventure story with logically sequenced events and resolution.

Success criteria
- I can plan characters and settings.
- I can plan a story outline.
- I can write a story opening.
- I can use dialogue.
- I can make a story exciting.
- I can write a story ending.

Setting the context
This activity should be carried out once children have completed Narrative Unit 3. Gather the children's work that has been done on writing a new adventure story during the course of the unit, such as: a new character outline, letter written in role, story plans and dialogue. Invite the children to briefly look back at their work and then to tell you, a classmate or the group their adventure story orally.

Assessment opportunity
The children should be given sufficient time to allow them to think about, make notes on and remember their ideas before telling the story. This activity provides an opportunity to assess the children's understanding of the work they have completed in the course of the unit and their ability to put it into practice to create an effective adventure story. Make notes of the children's responses.

Assessment evidence
In this activity, children tell their adventure stories orally. Make a note of your comments and use these as evidence towards Writing AF3. Children working at levels 2-3 will organise their ideas logically, with clear sequencing and attempts at creating effective openings and endings. Children working at levels 4-5 will ensure that the material is more carefully structured from start to finish, developing their material clearly. There will be clear links between each stage and echoes between stages, making a cohesive whole. Use this activity as well as examples of children's work throughout this unit to make level judgements for Writing.

Name	Date

Typical characters (1)

Adventure-story characters

My favourite character is _____

from _____

by _____

■ What happens to the character in the story?

_____

_____

_____

_____

_____

_____

_____

_____

■ Circle the adjectives that could describe your favourite character.

brave	shy	strong	daring
silly	clever	timid	frightened	curious
funny	inventive	serious	clumsy
naughty	kind	fearless	lazy	weak

Red
Amber
Green

I can identify features of an adventure-story character. ☐

NARRATIVE

Name

Date

Planning a character

Family

Home

Main character

My main character

Appearance

Personality

I can plan a character for an adventure story. ☐

Red
Amber
Green

PHOTOCOPIABLE ■SCHOLASTIC

Name   Date

Write a letter

Your address

_____

_____

_____

_____

Dear _____

How are you? You'll never believe what happened!!

_____

_____

_____

_____

_____

I can't wait to find out what happens next! I'll let you know.

Love from

_____

Red
Amber   I can describe an event using the first person. ☐
Green

NARRATIVE
UNIT 4 Authors and letters

Literacy objectives

Speak and listen for a wide range of purposes in different contexts
Strand 1 Speaking
- Sustain conversation, explain or give reasons for their views or choices.

Strand 3 Group discussion and interaction
- Use talk to organise roles and action.
- Actively include and respond to all members of the group.

Read and write for a range of purposes on paper and on screen
Strand 7 Understanding and interpreting texts
- Explore how different texts appeal to readers using varied sentence structures and descriptive language.

Strand 8 Engaging with and responding to texts
- Share and compare reasons for reading preferences, extending the range of books read.
- Identify features that writers use to provoke readers' reactions.

Strand 9 Creating and shaping texts
- Use layout, format, graphics and illustrations for different purposes.

Strand 10 Text structure and organisation
- Group related material into paragraphs.

Strand 11 Sentence structure and punctuation
- Compose sentences using adjectives, verbs and nouns for precision, clarity and impact.

Strand 12 Presentation
- Write with consistency in the size and proportion of letters and spacing within and between words, using the correct formation of handwriting joins.
- Develop accuracy and speed when using keyboard skills to type, edit and re-draft.

Key aspects of learning

Reasoning
- Children will learn about gathering evidence to support their opinions about books and giving reasons when they state their point of view to the class.

Self-awareness
- Children will discuss and reflect on their personal responses to texts read.

Social skills
- When working collaboratively, children will listen to and respect other people's ideas.

Communication
- Children will communicate outcomes orally, in writing and through ICT if appropriate.

Assessment focuses

Reading
AF4 (identify and comment on the structure and organisation of texts, including grammatical and presentational features at text level).
AF6 (identify and comment on writers' purposes and viewpoints, and the overall effect of the text on the reader).
AF7 (relate texts to their social, cultural and historical contexts and literary traditions).

Writing
AF2 (produce texts which are appropriate to task, reader and purpose).
AF3 (organise and present whole texts effectively, sequencing and structuring information, ideas and events).

Speaking and listening
Speaking (speak with clarity, intonation and pace).
Group discussion and interaction (support others, take turns).

Resources

Phase 1
Photocopiable page, 'Author study' (versions 1 and 2)
Photocopiable page, 'Book review'
Phase 2
Photocopiable page, 'Dear author'
Interactive activity, 'Dear author'
Photocopiable page, 'Formal or informal?'
Interactive activity, 'Formal or informal?'
Periodic assessment
Photocopiable page, 'Narrative 4 Reading assessment'

Unit 4 🔲 Authors and letters

Learning outcomes	Assessment opportunity and evidence	Assessment focuses (AFs)		Success criteria
		Level 2	Level 3	
Phase ① activities pages 71-72				
Author study Children can explain why they like books by a particular author, referring to an author's style or themes.	● Supported group discussion where children compare books by two authors. ● Children's discussions and notes on their oral responses.	**Reading AF6** ● Some awareness that writers have viewpoints and purposes. ● Simple statements about likes and dislikes in reading, sometimes with reasons.	**Reading AF6** ● Comments identify main purpose. ● Express personal response but with little awareness of writer's viewpoint or effect on reader.	● I can compare two books by an author. ● I can describe an author's style of writing.
Book reviews Children can explain why they like books by a particular author, referring to an author's style or themes.	● Supported group activity where children write a book review. ● Children's discussions and notes on their oral responses.	**Reading AF6** ● Some awareness that writers have viewpoints and purposes. ● Simple statements about likes and dislikes in reading, sometimes with reasons. **Writing AF2** ● Some basic purpose established. ● Some appropriate features of the given form used. ● Some attempts to adopt appropriate style.	**Reading AF6** ● Comments identify main purpose. ● Express personal response but with little awareness of writer's viewpoint or effect on reader. **Writing AF2** ● Purpose established at a general level. ● Main features of selected form sometimes signalled to the reader. ● Some attempts at appropriate style, with attention to reader.	● I can write a book review. ● I can explain why I liked a book.
Phase ② activities pages 73-74				
Dear author (1) Children can identify the key features of different types of letter.	● Supported group activity where children re-order sections of a letter. ● Children's sequenced letters on paper or in the interactive activity.	**Reading AF4** ● Some awareness of use of features of organisation.	**Reading AF4** ● A few basic features of organisation at text level identified, with little or no linked comment.	I can understand how letters are structured.
Formal or informal? Children can identify the key features of different types of letter.	● Independent activity where children identify formal/informal letters. ● Children's oral and written responses.	**Reading AF7** ● General features of a few text types identified. ● Some awareness that books are set in different times and places.	**Reading AF7** ● Some simple connections between texts identified. ● Recognition of some features of the context of texts.	I can understand the difference between formal and informal letters.
Phase ③ activities pages 74-75				
Dear author (2) Children can write a letter for a specific purpose and audience.	● Supported group activity where children write a letter to an author. ● Children's oral and written responses.	**Writing AF3** ● Some basic sequencing of ideas or material. ● Openings and/or closings sometimes signalled.	**Writing AF3** ● Some attempt to organise ideas with related points placed next to each other. ● Openings and closings usually signalled. ● Some attempt to sequence ideas or material logically.	I can write a letter to an author.
Dear friend Children can write a letter for a specific purpose and audience.	● Supported group activity where children write a letter to a friend. ● Children's written responses, and observational notes.	**Writing AF3** ● Some basic sequencing of ideas or material. ● Openings and/or closings sometimes signalled.	**Writing AF3** ● Some attempt to organise ideas with related points placed next to each other. ● Openings and closings usually signalled. ● Some attempt to sequence ideas or material logically.	I can write a letter to a friend.

Unit 4 ▢ Authors and letters

Learning outcomes	Assessment opportunity and evidence	Assessment focuses (AFs)		Success criteria
		Level 4	Level 5	
Phase ① activities pages 71-72				
Author study Children can explain why they like books by a particular author, referring to an author's style or themes.	• Group discussion where children compare books by two authors. • Children's discussions and notes on their oral responses.	**Reading AF6** • Main purpose identified. • Simple comments show some awareness of writer's viewpoint. • Simple comment on overall effect on reader.	**Reading AF6** • Main purpose clearly identified, often through general overview. • Viewpoint in texts clearly identified, with some, often limited, explanation. • General awareness of effect on the reader, with some, often limited explanation.	• I can compare two books by an author. • I can describe an author's style of writing.
Book reviews Children can explain why they like books by a particular author, referring to an author's style or themes.	• Independent activity where children write a book review. • Children's discussions and notes on their oral responses.	**Reading AF6** • Main purpose identified. • Simple comments show some awareness of writer's viewpoint. • Simple comment on overall effect on reader. **Writing AF2** • Main purpose of writing is clear but not always consistently maintained. • Main features of selected form are clear and appropriate to purpose. • Style generally appropriate to task, though awareness of reader not always sustained.	**Reading AF6** • Main purpose clearly identified, often through general overview. • Viewpoint in texts clearly identified, with some, often limited, explanation. • General awareness of effect on the reader, with some, often limited, explanation. **Writing AF2** • Main purpose of writing is clear and consistently maintained. • Features of selected form clearly established with some adaptation to purpose. • Appropriate style clearly established to maintain reader's interest throughout.	• I can write a book review • I can explain why I liked a book.
Phase ② activities pages 73-74				
Dear author (1) Children can identify the key features of different types of letter.	• Paired activity where children re-order sections of a letter. • Children's sequenced letters on paper or in the interactive activity.	**Reading AF4** • Some structural choices identified with simple comment. • Some basic features of organisation at text level identified.	**Reading AF4** • Comments on structural choices show some general awareness of writer's craft. • Various features relating to organisation at text level, including form, are clearly identified, with some explanation.	I can understand how letters are structured.
Formal or informal? Children can identify the key features of different types of letter.	• Independent activity where children identify formal/informal letters. • Children's oral responses and completed interactive activity.	**Reading AF7** • Features common to different texts or versions of the same text identified, with simple comment. • Simple comment on the effect that the reader's or writer's context has on the meaning of texts.	**Reading AF7** • Comments identify similarities and differences between texts, or versions, with some explanation. • Some explanation of how the contexts in which texts are written and read contribute to meaning.	I can understand the difference between formal and informal letters.

Unit 4 ☐ Authors and letters

Learning outcomes	Assessment opportunity and evidence	Assessment focuses (AFs)		Success criteria
		Level 4	Level 5	
Phase ③ activities pages 74-75				
Dear author (2) Children can write a letter for a specific purpose and audience.	• Independent activity where children write a letter to an author. • Children's oral and written responses.	**Writing AF3** • Ideas organised by clustering related points or by time sequence • Ideas are organised simply with a fitting opening and closing, sometimes linked. • Ideas or material generally in logical sequence but overall direction of writing not always clearly signalled.	**Writing AF3** • Material is structured clearly, with sentences organised into appropriate paragraphs. • Development of material is effectively managed across text. • Overall direction of the text supported by clear links between paragraphs.	I can write a letter to an author.
Dear friend Children can write a letter for a specific purpose and audience.	• Independent activity where children write a letter to a friend. • Children's written responses.	**Writing AF3** • Ideas organised by clustering related points or by time sequence. • Ideas are organised simply with a fitting opening and closing, sometimes linked. • Ideas or material generally in logical sequence but overall direction of writing not always clearly signalled.	**Writing AF3** • Material is structured clearly, with sentences organised into appropriate paragraphs. • Development of material is effectively managed across text. • Overall direction of the text supported by clear links between paragraphs.	I can write a letter to a friend.

Phase ① Author study

Learning outcome
Children can explain why they like books by a particular author, referring to an author's style or themes.

Success criteria
- I can compare two books by an author.
- I can describe an author's style of writing.

Setting the context
This activity should be carried out once the children have read more than one story written by the same author, for example, Dick King-Smith, Malorie Blackman or Mary Hoffman. Ensure the children have had experience of comparing work by an author in terms of subject matter, style and theme in shared and guided reading and through group discussions. Provide the children with copies of the photocopiable page 'Author study' (versions 1 and 2). Children working at levels 2–3 should use version 1 of the photocopiable page while the children working at levels 4–5 should use version 2. They should draw comparisons between two stories written by an author of their choice or an author the class has been studying.

Assessment opportunity
Children working at levels 2–3 work in a supported discussion group. An adult can ask questions to draw out the children's responses, for example: *Are the themes of both stories the same or different? Is the story about 'wishing to be different' or 'wishing to be the same as others'? Does the story make you laugh, feel sad or excited? Can you think of an adjective to describe the style of the story?* Children working at levels 4–5 will work in small groups. When they have completed the activity they discuss and compare their opinions of the chosen author.

Assessment evidence
At levels 2–3, children will identify the main events in the stories and will pick an adjective to describe the style of each one. However the group discussions will reveal their lack of awareness of the author's viewpoint and purposes. At levels 4–5, children will be able to describe the writing style using their own words. They will demonstrate an awareness of the author's viewpoint and its effect on the reader, explaining easily the reasons why they like this author's writing. Use the children's written responses and the notes made during the group discussion to provide evidence for Reading AF6.

Next steps
Support: Provide children with sticky notes with 'funny', 'sad', 'exciting' and so on written on them and a selection of stories that they have read in guided and personal reading. Ask them to label the books.
Extension: Ask children to give an oral assessment of an author's work to others in the class.

Key aspects of learning
Reasoning: Children will learn about gathering evidence to support their opinions about books and giving reasons when they state their point of view to the class.
Self-awareness: Children will discuss and reflect on their personal responses to texts read.
Social skills: When working collaboratively, children will listen to and respect other people's ideas.
Communication: Children will communicate outcomes orally, in writing and through ICT if appropriate.

NARRATIVE

Phase ① Book reviews

Learning outcome
Children can explain why they like books by a particular author, referring to an author's style or themes.

Success criteria
- I can write a book review.
- I can explain why I liked a book.

Setting the context
This activity should be undertaken after the children have read and discussed a shared book, either as a class or as a group. The children should have engaged in teacher- or adult-led discussions using prompts such as: *Which parts of the plot were the most exciting? Why? Who was the most interesting character? What made them interesting? How did the author keep the reader's attention? What parts of the story reminded you of experiences you have been through? What is the author trying to say to the reader? Who would you recommend this book to?* Children work in small groups to discuss the book. Then provide them with copies of the photocopiable page 'Book review' and invite them to write their own book review.

Assessment opportunity
Make notes of the children's oral responses during class or group discussions. Children working at levels 2–3 work in a supported group using the prompts from the previous discussions. An adult can make notes of the children's responses. The children can then complete the photocopiable page independently after discussion. Children working at levels 4–5 complete the photocopiable page independently.

Assessment evidence
At levels 2–3, children will identify the book's subject and give a personal response. Since they may be unable to explain their response, they will find it difficult to suggest who else might enjoy the book. Their writing will otherwise be fit for purpose and appropriate in style. At levels 4–5, children will show greater awareness of the effects of the book on themselves and others. The purpose of their review will be clear and their consistent style will maintain readers' interest. Use the completed sheet and observational notes to provide evidence for Reading AF6 and Writing AF2.

Next steps
Support: Send a book-review writing frame home with the reading books of those who struggled to write a book review, to give them further practice.
Extension: Invite children to present their book review to the class. Encourage others to evaluate the book review.

Key aspects of learning
Reasoning: Children will learn about gathering evidence to support their opinions about books and giving reasons when they state their point of view to the class.
Self-awareness: Children will discuss and reflect on their personal responses to texts read.
Social skills: When working collaboratively, children will listen to and respect other people's ideas.
Communication: Children will communicate outcomes orally, in writing and through ICT if appropriate.

Phase ② Dear author (1)

Learning outcome
Children can identify the key features of different types of letter.

Success criteria
I can understand how letters are structured.

Setting the context
This activity should be undertaken after the children have explored the features of letters written for different purposes in modelled, shared and guided reading and writing, with the class and in groups. They should have explored the conventions of layout and language, including punctuation. The children sequence a letter written to an author to describe why they enjoyed a particular book. They use photocopiable page 'Dear author', cut out the sections and re-order them into a logical sequence, or use the interactive activity 'Dear author'.

Assessment opportunity
Children working at levels 2–3 can either work in a supported group and discuss the order as they collaborate to re-order the sections, or undertake the interactive activity independently. Children working at levels 4–5 should work with a partner when using the photocopiable cut-out sections of a letter.

Assessment evidence
At levels 2–3, children will have a basic knowledge of how a letter is put together. They will know the positions of the address, greeting and signature, but may be a little less clear on the organisation of the main body. At levels 4–5, children will be better able to make structural choices as they put together the main part of the letter. Use the completed activities to provide evidence towards Reading AF4.

Next steps
Support: Provide a letter writing frame and invite children to write a letter to an author.
Extension: Children write their own letters to an author independently.

Key aspects of learning
Social skills: When working collaboratively, children will listen to and respect other people's ideas.
Communication: Children will develop their ability to discuss as they work collaboratively in paired, group and whole-class contexts. They will communicate outcomes orally, in writing and through ICT if appropriate.

Phase ② Formal or informal?

Learning outcome
Children can identify the key features of different types of letter.

Success criteria
I can understand the difference between formal and informal letters.

Setting the context
This activity should be undertaken after the children have explored the typical layout of formal letters and the different types of language that are used in formal and informal letters. They will have explored the language conventions of formal letters, such as letters to complain, to inform and to persuade. They will have discussed in shared and guided groups how the purpose and the audience of letters affect the choice of language in letters. Children working at levels 2–3 are given copies of the photocopiable page 'Formal or informal?' and asked to identify which sentences and phrases are from a formal or an informal letter. Children working at levels 4–5 work on the interactive activity 'Formal or informal?'.

▷ **Assessment opportunity**
Working in small discussion groups, the children explore and compare the language styles of formal and informal letters and the reasons why they are different. A supporting adult can make notes of the children's responses. The children independently complete the photocopiable page or the interactive activity.

Assessment evidence
At levels 2-3, children will recognise the key features of a letter and will show an awareness of the different contexts in which a letter might be written. They may be less successful in classifying all the phrases correctly. At levels 4-5, children will have a greater appreciation of the links between context and content and are more likely to label correctly the phrases that are less common. Use the completed activities and any observational notes to provide evidence towards Reading AF7.

Next steps
Support: Create a 'compare and contrast' display of formal and informal.
Extension: Children collect different examples of formal language and record them in reading journals.

Key aspects of learning
Self-awareness: Children will discuss and reflect on their personal responses to texts read.
Social skills: When working collaboratively, children will listen to and respect other people's ideas.
Communication: As they learn the conventions of letter writing, children will begin to appreciate the need to vary tone and content according to audience and purpose. They will communicate outcomes orally, in writing and through ICT if appropriate.

Phase ③ Dear author (2)

Learning outcome
Children can write a letter for a specific purpose and audience.

Success criteria
I can write a letter to an author.

Setting the context
This activity should be undertaken after the children have analysed the language and layout of different forms of letter. They should have begun to develop an awareness of how audience and purpose can affect language choices. They should have explored how to compose a letter to an author during modelled, shared and guided writing sessions. They should have read and compared stories written by one particular author and evaluated his or her work. Invite the children to compose real letters to send to the author for a specified purpose, for example, to express their opinions or to ask for information.

Assessment opportunity
Children working at levels 2-3 work in small groups with a supporting adult to discuss their ideas, letter layout and language. An adult working with the group can make notes of their ideas . The children then write a polished version of their letter. Give time to children working at levels 4-5 to discuss and plan the content of their letters, and experiment with different words and phrases in pairs. They then write a polished version.

Assessment evidence
At levels 2-3, children will sequence their writing logically and write appropriate lines to begin and end the letter. At levels 4-5, children will deliberately structure the letter, clearly developing their ideas in stages and using paragraphs to delineate them. The overall direction of the text will be clear and there may be some links between the opening and closing points. Use the children's written responses, and any observational notes, to provide evidence towards Writing AF3.

Next steps
Support: Provide examples of sentences to use as models.
Extension: Ask children to write a letter both to express an opinion and to request information.

Key aspects of learning
Reasoning: Children will learn about gathering evidence to support their opinions about books and giving reasons when they state their point of view.
Social skills: When working collaboratively, children will listen to and respect other people's ideas.
Communication: As they learn the conventions of letter writing, children will begin to appreciate the need to vary tone and content according to audience and purpose. They will communicate outcomes orally, in writing and through ICT if appropriate.

Phase ③ Dear friend

Learning outcome
Children can write a letter for a specific purpose and audience.

Success criteria
I can write a letter to a friend.

Setting the context
This activity should be undertaken after the children have analysed the language and layout of different forms of letter. They should have begun to develop an awareness of how audience and purpose can affect language choices. They will have explored how to compose a letter and should have also written book reviews. Invite the children to compose real letters to send to a friend for a specified purpose, perhaps to recommend a book they have enjoyed.

Assessment opportunity
Children working at levels 2-3 work in a supported group. An adult can ask questions to draw out their responses, for example: *You know your friend well, so how do you think you should open the letter? How will your friend know which book you want him or her to read? What are the best points about the book? Don't forget you want him or her to read the book, so how much detail about the plot do you think you should include? How do you want to sign off the letter?* Children working at levels 4-5 should work independently to write their letters.

Assessment evidence
At levels 2-3, children will sequence their writing logically and write appropriate lines to begin and end the letter. At levels 4-5, children will deliberately (if informally) structure the letter, clearly developing their ideas in stages and using paragraphs to delineate them. The overall direction of the text will be clear and there may be some links between the opening and closing points. Use the children's written responses, and any observational notes as evidence towards Writing AF3.

Next steps
Support: Ask those who struggled to write a letter to recommend a book, to write a letter inviting a friend to visit.
Extension: Have children write a letter to a child in another class whom they only know slightly, and compare the level of informality in the tone.

Key aspects of learning
Reasoning: Children will learn about gathering evidence to support their opinions about books and giving reasons when they state their point of view.
Social skills: When working collaboratively, children will listen to and respect other people's ideas.
Communication: As they learn the conventions of letter writing, children will begin to appreciate the need to vary tone and content according to audience and purpose. They will communicate outcomes orally, in writing and through ICT if appropriate.

Periodic assessment

Reading

Learning outcome Children can identify the key features of different types of letter.	**Success criteria** I can understand the difference between formal and informal letters. **Setting the context** This activity should be carried out once children have completed Narrative Unit 4. Provide the children with copies of the photocopiable page 'Narrative 4 Reading assessment' and invite them to read the letter extracts and decide by their language and tone if they are from formal or informal letters to a known or unknown audience. Ask them to explain their answers orally by identifying words and phrases that indicate the level of formality and the audience. **Assessment opportunity** Assess the children's ability to understand how audience and purpose affects a writer's choice of language and tone. Make notes on their oral responses. **Assessment evidence** Use the children's written responses, and any observation notes, to provide evidence towards Reading AF5. At levels 2–3, children will identify the 'Dear Sir' letter as formal but may find difficult those that are less clear-cut. They may also find confusing the fact that formal letters are sometimes written to known people. At levels 4–5, children will show more understanding of the different authorial voices and will be more successful at spotting the language features of a formal letter.

Writing

Learning outcome Children can explain why they like books by a particular author referring to an author's style or themes.	**Success criteria** ● I can present a book review. ● I can explain why I like a particular book. **Setting the context** This activity should be carried out once the children have completed Narrative Unit 4. Invite the children to choose a book they have not written a review for and give an oral book review for the class. **Assessment opportunity** Give the children time to make notes for their oral book review. Children working at levels 2–3 can use a previously written book review to present to the class. Assess the children's ability to use language orally to inform a known audience. Encourage them to ask questions and to say if the review has given them sufficient information to entice them into reading the book. **Assessment evidence** Use the children's oral book reviews, and any observational notes, to provide evidence towards Writing AF2. At levels 2–3, children will be aware of the main features of book reviews and in general they will follow the accepted model. At levels 4–5, the purpose of the children's oral book reviews will be clear. The style of their notes and oral presentations will be appropriate to task although their attempts to engage the audience may not be sustained.

Name   Date

Author study (1)

Author name: _____

Title:	Title:
Setting:	Setting:
Main character:	Main character:
What happens in the story?	What happens in the story?
Circle a word to describe the style of the story: funny exciting scary sad happy mysterious	Circle a word to describe the style of the story: funny exciting scary sad happy mysterious
Colour in the stars to rate this story: ☆☆☆☆☆	Colour in the stars to rate this story: ☆☆☆☆☆

Red
Amber
Green

I can compare two books by an author. ☐
I can describe an author's style of writing. ☐

NARRATIVE

Name   Date

Book review

Title:

Author:

What the book is about:

What I enjoyed about this book:

Who else would enjoy this book:

Score: ☆ ☆ ☆ ☆ ☆

Red
Amber
Green

I can write a book review. ☐

I can explain why I liked a book. ☐

Name	Date

Formal or informal?

◾ Would you write these phrases and sentences in a formal letter or an informal letter?

◾ Shade the backgrounds red for formal and blue for informal.

Dear Sir,

Hi!

All the best,

Dear Mrs Browning,

Yours faithfully,

Yours sincerely,

Lots of love,

See you soon,

Sorry but I can't come – such a pity!

I am writing to inform you

Red
Amber
Green

I can understand the difference between formal and informal letters.

NARRATIVE
UNIT 5 Dialogue and plays

Literacy objectives

Speak and listen for a wide range of purposes in different contexts
Strand 1 Speaking
- Sustain conversation, explain or give reasons for their views or choices.

Strand 3 Group discussion and interaction
- Use talk to organise roles and action.
- Use the language of possibility to investigate and reflect on feelings, behaviour or relationships.

Strand 4 Drama
- Present events and characters through dialogue to engage the interest of an audience.
- Use some drama strategies to explore stories or issues.
- Identify and discuss qualities of others' performances, including gestures, action and costume.

Read and write for a range of purposes on paper and on screen
Strand 7 Understanding and interpreting texts
- Infer characters' feelings in fiction and consequences in logical explanations.

Strand 8 Engaging with and responding to texts
- Share and compare reasons for reading preferences, extending the range of books read.
- Empathise with characters and debate moral dilemmas portrayed in texts.
- Identify features that writers use to provoke readers' reactions.

Strand 9 Creating and shaping texts
- Make decisions about form and purpose, identify success criteria and use them to evaluate their writing.
- Select and use a range of technical and descriptive vocabulary.
- Use layout, format, graphics and illustrations for different purposes.

Strand 10 Text structure and organisation
- Signal sequence, place and time to give coherence.

Strand 11 Sentence structure and punctuation
- Show relationships of time, reason and cause through subordination and connectives.
- Compose sentences using adjectives, verbs and nouns for precision, clarity and impact.

Strand 12 Presentation
- Develop accuracy and speed when using keyboard skills to type, edit and re-draft.

Key aspects of learning

Creative thinking
- Use creative thinking to extend and consider alternatives to typical elements when writing, and create dialogue of their own.

Social skills
- When working collaboratively, children will listen to and respect other people's ideas.

Evaluation
- Express their own views and preferences against agreed success criteria.

Empathy
- Understand what others might be feeling in a particular situation.

Assessment focuses

Reading
AF4 *(identify and comment on the structure and organisation of texts, including grammatical and presentational features at text level).*

Writing
AF1 *(write imaginative, interesting and thoughtful texts).*
AF2 *(produce texts which are appropriate to task, reader and purpose).*
AF3 *(organise and present whole texts effectively, sequencing and structuring information, ideas and events).*
AF6 *(write with technical accuracy of syntax and punctuation in phrases, clauses and sentences).*
AF7 *(select appropriate and effective vocabulary).*

Speaking and listening
Speaking (speak with clarity, intonation and pace).
Group discussion and interaction (support others, take turns).
Drama (plan, perform and evaluate plays).

Resources

Phase 1
Photocopiable page, 'Speech punctuation'
Interactive activity, 'Speech punctuation'
Phase 2
Photocopiable page, 'Playscript features' (versions 1 and 2)
Phase 3
Photocopiable page, 'Story to play'
Interactive activity, 'Storyboard'
Photocopiable page, 'Jack and the Beanstalk'
Periodic assessment
Photocopiable page, 'Narrative 5 Reading assessment text'
Photocopiable page, 'Narrative 5 Reading assessment'
Photocopiable page, 'Narrative 5 Writing assessment text'
Photocopiable page, 'Narrative 5 Writing assessment'

Unit 5 ☐ Dialogue and plays

Learning outcomes	Assessment opportunity and evidence	Assessment focuses (AFs)		Success criteria
		Level 2	Level 3	
Phase ① activity page 85				
Speech punctuation Children can understand how the use and conventions of written dialogue differ between prose and playscripts.	• Supported group activity where children identify dialogue. • Children's interactive activity and written responses.	**Writing AF6** • Clause structure mostly grammatically correct. • Sentence demarcation with capital letters and full stops usually accurate. • Some accurate use of question and exclamation marks, and commas in lists.	**Writing AF6** • Straightforward sentences usually demarcated accurately with full stops, capital letters, question and exclamation marks. • Some, limited, use of speech punctuation. • Comma splicing evident, particularly in narrative.	I can understand how to punctuate dialogue.
Phase ② activities pages 85-86				
Playscript features Children can understand the conventions and features of playscript writing.	• Supported group activity where children identify playscript features. • Peer-evaluation of each other's writing. • Children's completed photocopiable pages, written responses.	**Reading AF4** • Some awareness of use of features of organisation. **Writing AF2** • Some basic purpose established. • Some appropriate features of the given form used. • Some attempts to adopt appropriate style.	**Reading AF4** • A few basic features of organisation at text level identified, with little or no linked comment. **Writing AF2** • Purpose established at a general level. • Main features of selected form sometimes signalled to the reader. • Some attempts at appropriate style, with attention to reader.	• I can understand the layout and features of a playscript. • I can identify stage directions. • I can write a new scene.
Phase ③ activities pages 86-89				
Story to play Children can plan, write and perform a play based on a well-known story.	• Supported group activity where children discuss and choose a title for a new play. • Children's written and oral responses.	**Reading AF4** • Some awareness of use of features of organisation.	**Reading AF4** • A few basic features of organisation at text level identified, with little or no linked comment.	• I can understand which stories will make a good play. • I can begin to plan a play by writing notes.
Storyboard Children can plan, write and perform a play based on a well-known story.	• Supported group activity where children create a storyboard. • Completed interactive activity and notes on children's oral responses.	**Writing AF3** • Some basic sequencing of ideas or material. • Openings and/or closings sometimes signalled.	**Writing AF3** • Some attempt to organise ideas with related points placed next to each other. • Openings and closings usually signalled. • Some attempt to sequence ideas or material logically.	I can plan a play using storyboards.
New scene Children can plan, write and perform a play based on a well-known story.	• Supported group activity where children plan a new scene for a playscript. • Children's oral and written responses and their own evaluations.	**Writing AF1** • Mostly relevant ideas and content, sometimes repetitive or sparse. • Some apt word choices create interest. • Brief comments, questions about events or actions suggest viewpoint.	**Writing AF1** • Some appropriate ideas and content included. • Some attempt to elaborate on basic information or events. • Attempt to adopt viewpoint, though often not maintained or inconsistent.	I can write a playscript.
Stage directions Children can plan, write and perform a play based on a well-known story.	• Paired activity where children add stage directions to dialogue. • Children's oral responses and the completed interactive activity.	**Writing AF7** • Simple, often speech-like vocabulary conveys relevant meanings. • Some adventurous word choices.	**Writing AF7** • Simple, generally appropriate vocabulary used, limited in range. • Some words selected for effect or occasion.	I can add stage directions to a playscript.

Unit 5 Dialogue and plays

NARRATIVE

Learning outcomes	Assessment opportunity and evidence	Assessment focuses (AFs)		Success criteria
		Level 4	**Level 5**	
Phase ① activity page 85				
Speech punctuation Children can understand how the use and conventions of written dialogue differ between prose and playscripts.	• Independent activity where children identify dialogue. • Children's interactive activity and written responses.	**Writing AF6** • Sentences demarcated accurately throughout the text, including question marks. • Speech marks to denote speech generally accurate, with some other speech punctuation. • Commas used in lists and occasionally to mark clauses, although not always accurately.	**Writing AF6** • Full range of punctuation used accurately to demarcate sentences, including speech punctuation. • Syntax and punctuation within the sentence generally accurate including commas to mark clauses, though some errors occur where ambitious structures are attempted.	I can understand how to punctuate dialogue.
Phase ② activities pages 85-86				
Playscript features Children can understand the conventions and features of playscript writing.	• Paired activity where children identify playscript features. • Peer-evaluation of each other's writing. • Children's completed photocopiable pages, written responses.	**Reading AF4** • Some structural choices identified with simple comment. • Some basic features of organisation at text level identified. **Writing AF2** • Main purpose of writing is clear but not always consistently maintained. • Main features of selected form are clear and appropriate to purpose. • Style generally appropriate to task, though awareness of reader not always sustained.	**Reading AF4** • Comments on structural choices show some general awareness of writer's craft. • Various features relating to organisation at text level, including form, are clearly identified, with some explanation. **Writing AF2** • Main purpose of writing is clear and consistently maintained. • Features of selected form clearly established with some adaptation to purpose. • Appropriate style clearly established to maintain reader's interest throughout.	• I can understand the layout and features of a playscript. • I can identify stage directions. • I can write a new scene.
Phase ③ activities pages 86-89				
Story to play Children can plan, write and perform a play based on a well-known story.	• Independent activity where children discuss and choose a title for a new play. • Children's written and oral responses.	**Reading AF4** • Some structural choices identified with simple comment. • Some basic features of organisation at text level identified.	**Reading AF4** • Comments on structural choices show some general awareness of writer's craft. • Various features relating to organisation at text level, including form, are clearly identified, with some explanation.	• I can understand which stories will make a good play. • I can begin to plan a play by writing notes.
Storyboard Children can plan, write and perform a play based on a well-known story.	• Paired activity where children create a storyboard. • Completed interactive activity and notes on children's oral responses.	**Writing AF3** • Ideas organised by clustering related points or by time sequence • Ideas are organised simply with a fitting opening and closing, sometimes linked. • Ideas or material generally in logical sequence but overall direction of writing not always clearly signalled.	**Writing AF3** • Material is structured clearly, with sentences organised into appropriate paragraphs. • Development of material is effectively managed across text. • Overall direction of the text supported by clear links between paragraphs.	I can plan a play using storyboards.

SCHOLASTIC

100 LITERACY ASSESSMENT LESSONS · YEAR 3   83

Unit 5 ⬜ Dialogue and plays

Learning outcomes	Assessment opportunity and evidence	Assessment focuses (AFs)		Success criteria
		Level 4	Level 5	
New scene Children can plan, write and perform a play based on a well-known story.	• Independent activity where children plan a new scene for a playscript. • Peer-evaluation. • Children's oral and written responses and their own evaluations.	**Writing AF1** • Relevant ideas and content chosen. • Some ideas and material developed in detail. • Straightforward viewpoint generally established and maintained.	**Writing AF1** • Relevant ideas and material developed with some imaginative detail. • Development of ideas and material appropriately shaped for selected form. • Clear viewpoint established, generally consistent, with some elaboration.	I can write a playscript.
Stage directions Children can plan, write and perform a play based on a well-known story.	• Paired activity where children add stage directions to dialogue. • Children's oral responses and the completed interactive activity.	**Writing AF7** • Some evidence of deliberate vocabulary choices. • Some expansion of general vocabulary to match topic.	**Writing AF7** • Vocabulary chosen for effect. • Reasonably wide vocabulary used, though not always appropriately.	I can add stage directions to a playscript.

Phase ① Speech punctuation

Learning outcome
Children can understand how the use and conventions of written dialogue differ between prose and playscripts.

Success criteria
I can understand how to punctuate dialogue.

Setting the context
The children should have previously explored several examples of dialogue in stories. They should have identified where speech marks are placed and the conventions of using commas, question marks and exclamation marks before the reporting clause (speech verb phrase), as well as punctuation when the reporting clause is written between one set of spoken words. Begin by reading the passage on 'Speech punctuation' from the photocopiable page to the whole class.

Assessment opportunity
After reading the passage to the whole class, invite children working at levels 2–3 to work in a supported group. They will identify the spoken words on interactive activity 'Speech punctuation' before adding the missing speech marks on the photocopiable page. Children working at levels 4–5 will work on the same task independently. Assess whether the children are secure in their understanding of speech punctuation.

Assessment evidence
At levels 2–3, children will have limited success in punctuating speech – despite their secure knowledge and use of sentence punctuation. At levels 4–5, children will generally use speech punctuation correctly. Use the children's written responses and the completed interactive activity to provide evidence for Writing AF6.

Next steps
Support: Use the passage on the photocopiable page and other dialogue extracts from well-known stories in small-group role play for those children who are insecure about punctuating dialogue and identifying spoken words in text.
Extension: Invite the children to add extra dialogue to the photocopiable page.

Key aspects of learning
Creative thinking: Use creative thinking to extend and consider alternatives to typical elements when writing, and create dialogue of their own.
Social skills: When working collaboratively, children will listen to and respect other people's ideas.

Phase ② Playscript features

Learning outcome
Children can understand the conventions and features of playscript writing.

Success criteria
● I can understand the layout and features of a playscript.
● I can identify stage directions.
● I can write a new scene.

Setting the context
The children should have previously discussed and analysed playscripts. They should have had opportunities to become familiar with the conventions and layout of playscripts including the cast list, scenes, how to differentiate between cast names and their spoken words (lines) and stage directions. Distribute the photocopiable page 'Playscript features' (versions 1 and 2) and ask children to annotate the text to label the features. Provide children working at levels 2–3 with version 1, and those working at levels 4–5 with version 2. When they have annotated the page, invite them to write a new scene for the play.

NARRATIVE

▷ **Assessment opportunity**

Children working at levels 2-3 work in a supported group. An adult can ask questions to draw out children's responses, for example: *Where is the next scene to be set? How do we tell the actors in the play about the setting? Do we need a cast list for a new scene? Who speaks first? Where should you write the character's name? Do you think you should tell any of the actors how to say their lines?* The supporting adult can make notes on individual children's responses. Invite some of the pairs to swap and read playscripts. Ask questions to encourage them to comment on the effectiveness of the playscripts: *Was it easy to read and understand? Could you act out the play as it has been written? What might be needed to improve it?* Children working at levels 4-5 complete the photocopiable page with a partner.

Assessment evidence

At levels 2-3, children will identify correctly most of the features listed and understand their purposes. However, they are unlikely to comment on them further. At levels 4-5, children will identify the features independently and in discussion they will show more awareness of how they are adapted to purpose. For example, the Wolf and Little Red exit in different directions because the Wolf doesn't want her to guess that he might follow her. Use the children's completed sheets, and your observational notes to provide evidence for Reading AF4 and Writing AF2.

Next steps

Support: Encourage children, when they are writing dialogue, to role play the scene beforehand.
Extension: Invite children to write a playscript for another traditional tale such as 'Goldilocks and the Three Bears'.

Key aspects of learning

Evaluation: Express their own views and preferences against agreed success criteria.
Creative thinking: Use creative thinking to extend and consider alternatives to typical elements when writing, and create dialogue of their own.
Social skills: When working collaboratively, children will listen to and respect other people's ideas.

Phase ③ Story to play

Learning outcome
Children can plan, write and perform a play based on a well-known story.

Success criteria
● I can understand which stories will make a good play.
● I can begin to plan a play by writing notes.

Setting the context
The children should have previously read examples of plays and analysed the layout and language of playscripts. Provide the children with a list of stories and ask them to choose one to rewrite as a play. Discuss their choices with them and ask them to suggest reasons why some stories will make good plays and others will not. Read the sentences on the photocopiable page 'Story to play' to the children and discuss possible answers before inviting them to choose a title and write their own responses to explain their choice.

Assessment opportunity
Children working at levels 2-3 work in a supported group and collaborate to choose one title for a new play. They discuss answers to provide reasons for their choice and a supporting adult makes notes of their responses on the class list. Ask questions to help them choose a story, for example: *This story moves to lots of different settings. Do you think it would it be easy to show that in a play? Why do*

■SCHOLASTIC

you think that? How many characters would it be easy to write dialogue for in a play? Why? A supporting adult can make notes of individual children's responses. Children working at levels 4-5 complete the photocopiable page independently.

Assessment evidence
At levels 2-3, children will come up with the necessary factual information (title, setting and so on) but will find it more difficult to give reasons for their decisions. They may also find it difficult to predict the audience reaction. At levels 4-5, children will be able to explain and comment on their own choices. Use children's oral responses and the completed sheets to provide evidence towards Reading AF4.

Next steps
Support: Provide children with copies of different plays and ask them to complete the photocopiable page to analyse their effectiveness.
Extension: The children share and discuss each other's response sheets and vote on which ones they think will make good plays.

Key aspects of learning
Evaluation: Express their own views and preferences against agreed success criteria.
Creative thinking: Use creative thinking to extend and consider alternatives to typical elements when writing, and create dialogue of their own.
Social skills: When working collaboratively, children will listen to and respect other people's ideas.

Phase ③ Storyboard

Learning outcome
Children can plan, write and perform a play based on a well-known story.

Success criteria
I can plan a play using storyboards.

Setting the context
The children should have previously discussed different stories with a view to using one of them as a basis for a playscript. They should have explored how to plan stories and plays using a storyboard. Explain that on the interactive activity 'Storyboard' they will see several images from a story to be used as scenes for four different playscripts. They should work out what the images show and decide the order of the scenes. The children use the final screen, 'Little Red Riding Hood', and draw their own storyboard and add another scene.

Assessment opportunity
Children working at levels 2-3 work in a supported group to draw their own storyboard. The supporting adult will help them reach decisions about adding a new scene and make notes of individuals' responses. Children working at levels 4-5 work in pairs on the interactive activity to sequence the images and then independently draw their own storyboard, adding another scene to 'Little Red Riding Hood'.

Assessment evidence
Children working at levels 2-3 will attempt to organise their ideas and to sequence their material logically. Children working at levels 4-5 will structure their work more clearly, with clear and obvious progression between scenes. The scene that they add will be consistent with the rest of the story and will appear at the correct point in the existing sequence of scenes. Use the children's storyboards and your notes to provide evidence towards Writing AF3.

Next steps
Support: Provide sentence strips that describe key scenes in familiar stories for children to practise sequencing.

Unit 5 Dialogue and plays

Extension: Children create a storyboard for a new story to describe the scenes for a play.

Key aspects of learning
Evaluation: Express their own views and preferences against agreed success criteria.
Creative thinking: Use creative thinking to extend and consider alternatives to typical elements when writing, and create dialogue of their own.
Social skills: When working collaboratively, children will listen to and respect other people's ideas.

Phase ③ New scene

Learning outcome
Children can plan, write and perform a play based on a well-known story.

Success criteria
I can write a playscript.

Setting the context
The children should have previously written scenes for a class play. During a shared writing session, write a short scene for a playscript based on a simple familiar story, or use an enlarged copy of scene 2 from 'Jack and the Beanstalk' on the photocopiable page. Discuss the text with the children as it is written so far and ask them to suggest how the play could continue in another scene (remind them that there is no right or wrong answer). Ask the children to write a new scene to continue the playscript.

Assessment opportunity
Children working at levels 2-3 work in a supported group to discuss details of what happens and make suggestions for dialogue. A supporting adult can ask questions to draw out and deepen their responses, for example: *If your next scene is when Jack returns to get the harp, what will the giant say in this scene? Who do you want to speak first? Do you want the giant to say the same sort of thing as in the previous scene or something different? If your next scene is when Jack gets home, what do you think he will tell his mother? What might his mother say? Do you think this would be a good scene for the play? Why? Why not?* and so on. Take this opportunity to note comments on the children's responses. Children working at levels 4-5 write another scene for the playscript independently. You may want to invite children to read their playscripts aloud to the class so that their classmates feed back on two things that worked well and one thing that could be improved.

Assessment evidence
At levels 2-3, children will include some appropriate content though their ideas may be repetitive, inconsistent or sparse. At levels 4-5, children will structure their material logically and develop it more consistently as the script progresses. Clear links between different sections will make clear the overall direction of the text. Use the children's written responses to provide evidence for Writing AF1.

Next steps
Support: Provide a playscript frame in columns.
Extension: Children write a script for scene 1 of 'Jack and the Beanstalk'.

Key aspects of learning
Evaluation: Express their own views and preferences against agreed success criteria.
Empathy: Understand what others might be feeling in a particular situation.
Creative thinking: Use creative thinking to extend and consider alternatives to typical elements when writing, and create dialogue of their own.
Social skills: When working collaboratively, children will listen to and respect other people's ideas.

> **Communication:** Children will develop their ability to discuss as they work collaboratively in paired, group and whole-class contexts. They will communicate outcomes orally, in writing and through ICT if appropriate.

Phase ③ Stage directions

Learning outcome
Children can plan, write and perform a play based on a well-known story.

Success criteria
I can add stage directions to a playscript.

Setting the context
Run this activity once the children have explored the layout and conventions of playscripts, including how and when stage direction are used. Revisit the playscript scene on the photocopiable page 'Jack and the Beanstalk'. Highlight and discuss the two types of stage directions, such as those used to tell an actor how to say their lines and those that describe action or movement. Invite the children to do the interactive activity 'Stage directions' in pairs, adding stage directions from choices from the drop-down list.

Assessment opportunity
Observe pairs of children as they discuss which choice is the best from the options given in the drop-down list and ask them to give reasons for their choices. Make notes of their discussions and individual contributions.

Assessment evidence
At levels 2–3, children will use simple and effective vocabulary that is generally appropriate and may feature the occasional more adventurous word. At levels 4–5, children will draw upon a wider range of vocabulary, deliberately choosing more words for their particular effects. Use the children's oral contributions and the completed interactive activity to provide evidence for Writing AF7.

Next steps
Support: Ask children to role play the script in small groups so they read and respond to stage directions.
Extension: Invite children to add stage directions to a playscript or scenes they have written in the earlier part of the unit.

Key aspects of learning
Creative thinking: Use creative thinking to extend and consider alternatives to typical elements when writing, and create dialogue of their own.

NARRATIVE

Periodic assessment

Reading

Learning outcome
Children can explain how the use and conventions of written dialogue differ between prose and playscripts.

Success criteria
- I can understand how dialogue affects plot.
- I can identify characters and their dialogue.
- I can understand the layout and features of a playscript.

Setting the context
This assessment should be carried out once children have completed Narrative Unit 5. They will have explored dialogue and how it differs between prose and playscripts, including speech punctuation, speech verbs and playscript layout. They will have experienced how, during shared, guided and independent reading, dialogue is used to move a story along in prose and playscripts. Discuss individual children's achievements with them. Ask them to suggest what they found difficult about the work in the unit and what they found easy and compare their responses with the comments made in your notes. Provide the children with copies of the photocopiable pages, 'Narrative 5 Reading assessment text', and 'Narrative 5 Reading assessment', and invite them to read both extracts and answer the questions.

Assessment opportunity
The children should be given sufficient time to allow them to read and digest the two extracts and to annotate them before answering the questions. This activity will enable you to assess the children's ability to understand the conventions for writing dialogue in stories and how they differ when using dialogue in playscripts. You may also want to use this an opportunity to assess some children's ability to read the extracts aloud.

Assessment evidence
Use the children's annotated texts and completed assessment sheets to provide evidence for Reading AF2 and AF4. The children's ability to read the extracts aloud may also provide some evidence for Reading AF1. At levels 2–3, children will correctly identify the basic features of the texts. They will also be able to answer most of the questions related to content but are likely to find more difficult those requiring comparison between the two texts. At level 2, children will read a range of familiar words on sight and will make some successful attempts to decode longer or unfamiliar words. At level 3, children will draw on many strategies to read with fluency and expression. At levels 4–5, children will have more awareness of the writer's craft and a clearer idea of the differences between a dialogue and a playscript. They will be able to support their comments with textual examples as required. Use this activity as well as examples of children's work throughout this unit to make level judgements for Reading.

Periodic assessment

Writing

Learning outcome
Children can understand the conventions and features of playscript writing.

Success criteria
- I can plan a play.
- I can add stage directions.

Setting the context
This assessment should be carried out once the children have completed Narrative Unit 5. Collect the work that has been completed during the course of the unit and discuss individual children's achievements with them. Ask them to suggest what they found difficult about the work and what they found easy to accomplish. Provide them with copies of the photocopiable pages 'Narrative 5 Writing assessment text' and 'Narrative 5 Writing assessment'. Explain that they are to make notes on the page to show how to turn the story into a play for radio. Ensure the children understand how a play for radio differs from one that an audience watches; that sound as well as speech is needed to help listeners understand what is happening.

Assessment opportunity
The children should be given sufficient time to allow them to read and think about what is needed and what could be omitted from the story to create a play version of it, before beginning the assessment. This activity provides an opportunity to assess the children's understanding of the work they have completed in the course of the unit and for them to demonstrate their knowledge of the features and conventions of playscript writing. After annotating the page, ask the children to explain their annotations and describe what happens in the play version.

Assessment evidence
Use the children's written responses to provide evidence towards Writing AF1. At levels 2–3, children will include appropriate content based on the text provided. For the most part they will make the transitions necessary to turn the text into a radio play, but there may be lapses and inconsistencies. At levels 4–5, children will develop the text with the imaginative detail needed to turn it into an interesting play. Their treatment of the text will be more consistent and they will ensure that ideas are followed through as necessary. Use this activity as well as examples of children's work throughout this unit to make level judgements for Writing.

Name Date

NARRATIVE

Speech punctuation

■ Add the speech marks to the passage to show what the characters said.

Where are you off to this fine morning? said the wolf.

Little Red knew she shouldn't talk to strangers but she didn't want to be rude

so she replied, I am going to grandma's house.

Well, take care through the woods and be sure you don't talk to strangers,

he advised.

When Little Red went into Grandma's house she saw Grandma was in bed.

Hello Grandma, she said How are you today?

A little better, replied the wolf, who was wearing Grandma's bonnet.

Goodness me, Grandma! said Little Red,

What a deep voice you've got today!

The wolf smiled.

And goodness me, Grandma.

What big teeth you've got!

Just then the door opened.

That isn't Grandma. It's a wolf!

shouted the woodcutter as he ran into the house.

Oh no! yelled the wolf and ran straight out past Little Red and the

woodcutter.

That's funny. He did look a lot like Grandma! laughed Little Red.

Illustration © 2009 Anna Godwin

Red
Amber
Green

I can understand how to punctuate dialogue.

Name   Date

Playscript features (1)

🔲 Annotate the page to show the playscript features using the phrases in the box:

Little Red and the Wolf

Cast:
Little Red
The wolf
A woodcutter

Scene 1: A wood.

Enter Little Red.

Wolf: *(appearing from behind a tree)*

Where are you off to this fine morning?

Little Red: I'm going to Grandma's house.

Wolf: Well, take care through the woods and be sure you

don't talk to strangers.

Exit Wolf stage left.

Exit Little Red stage right.

the title of the play	list of characters	stage directions
	character's spoken words	

Illustrations © 2009, Anna Godwin.

Red
Amber
Green

I can understand the layout and features of a playscript. ⬜

I can identify stage directions. ⬜

NARRATIVE

Name   Date

Story to play

The title of my new play is _____

The setting is _____

I think the setting will be good for a play because _____

_____

_____

The number of people in the cast is _____

This is a good number for the cast because _____

_____

_____

The number of scenes is _____

This is a good number of scenes because _____

_____

_____

_____

Audiences will find this play is _____

_____

_____

_____

Red
Amber
Green

I can understand which stories will make a good play. ☐

I can begin to plan a play by writing notes. ☐

Jack and the Beanstalk

Scene 2

Inside the giant's castle. Jack is hiding in a cupboard.

Giant: Wife! Bring me my hen and my harp.

Wife: Here they are dear. Now don't stay

up too long.

Exit wife stage left.

Giant: Lay hen, lay.

Hen: *(laying an egg)* Squawk!

Giant: Sing harp, sing.

The harp plays and giant snores.

Jack: *(whispering)* Now's my chance!

Jack grabs the hen.

Hen: Master, Master. Thief!

Jack: I'm off!

Exit Jack stage left.

Illustration © 2009, Anna Godwin.

NARRATIVE

NON-FICTION
UNIT 1 Reports

Literacy objectives

Speak and listen for a wide range of purposes in different contexts

Strand 1 Speaking
- Explain process or present information, ensuring that items are clearly sequenced, relevant details are included and accounts are ended effectively.

Strand 2 Listening and responding
- Identify the presentational features used to communicate the main points in a broadcast.
- Identify key sections in an information broadcast, noting how the language used signals changes or transitions in focus.

Read and write for a range of purposes on paper and on screen

Strand 7 Understanding and interpreting texts
- Identify and make notes of the main points of section(s) of text.
- Identify how different texts are organised, including reference texts, magazines and leaflets, on paper and on screen.

Strand 8 Engaging with and responding to texts
- Identify features that writers use to provoke readers' reactions.

Strand 9 Creating and shaping texts
- Write non-narrative texts using structures of different text types.
- Select and use a range of technical and descriptive vocabulary.
- Use layout, format, graphics and illustrations for different purposes.

Strand 10 Text structure and organisation
- Signal sequence, place and time to give coherence.
- Group related material into paragraphs.

Strand 11 Sentence structure and punctuation
- Show relationships of time, reason and cause through subordination and connectives.
- Compose sentences using adjectives, verbs and nouns for precision, clarity and impact.
- Clarify meaning through the use of exclamation marks and speech marks.

Strand 12 Presentation
- Write with consistency in size and proporation of letters and spacing within and between words, using the correct formation of handwriting joins.

Key aspects of learning

Information processing
● Children will identify relevant information from a range of sources on paper and on screen.
Social skills
● When working collaboratively, children will listen to and respect other people's ideas.
Communication
● Children will develop their ability to discuss the content and presentation of the reports they are listening to, reading and writing. They will often work collaboratively in pairs and groups. They will communicate outcomes orally, in writing and through ICT.
Evaluation
● Children will present information orally and in writing. They will discuss success criteria, give feedback to others and judge the effectiveness of their own work.
Enquiry
● Children will ask questions arising from work in another area of the curriculum (for example, teeth and eating), research and then plan how to present the information effectively.

Assessment focuses

Reading
AF2 (understand, describe, select or retrieve information, events or ideas from texts and use quotation and reference to text).
AF4 (identify and comment on the structure and organisation of texts, including grammatical and presentational features at text level).
AF5 (explain and comment on writers' use of language, including grammatical and literary features at word and sentence level).

Writing
AF3 (organise and present whole texts effectively, sequencing and structuring information, ideas and events).

Speaking and listening:
Speaking (speak with clarity, intonation and pace).
Listening and responding (ask relevant questions and respond appropriately).

Resources

Phase 1
Interactive activity, 'Key points'
Photocopiable page, 'Key facts' (versions 1 and 2)
Photocopiable page, 'Report plan' (versions 1 and 2)
Phase 3
Photocopiable page, 'Finding out'
Interactive activity, 'Finding out'
Interactive activity, 'Captions and labels'
Phase 4
Photocopiable page, 'Non-chronological report' (versions 1 and 2)
Periodic assessment
Interactive activity, 'Non-fiction 1 Reading assessment'

Unit 1 ▦ Reports

Learning outcomes	Assessment opportunity and evidence	Assessment focuses (AFs)		Success criteria
		Level 2	Level 3	
Phase ① activities pages 101–103				
Key points Children demonstrate that they have understood information read from a book or screen by noting the main points.	● Supported group activity where children highlight key words in report text. ● Children's completed interactive activity and teacher's notes.	**Reading AF2** ● Some specific, straightforward information recalled. ● Generally clear idea of where to look for information.	**Reading AF2** ● Simple, most obvious points identified though there may also be some misunderstanding. ● Some comments include quotations from or references to text, but not always relevant.	I can identify key ideas in paragraphs.
Key facts Children demonstrate that they have understood information read from a book or screen by noting the main points.	● Supported group activity where children highlight key facts in report text. ● Children's written responses and teacher's notes.	**Reading AF2** ● Some specific, straightforward information recalled. ● Generally clear idea of where to look for information.	**Reading AF2** ● Simple, most obvious points identified though there may also be some misunderstanding. ● Some comments include quotations from or references to text, but not always relevant.	I can identify key facts.
Report plan Children demonstrate that they have understood information read from a book or screen by noting the main points.	● Supported group activity where children make notes on a graphic organiser for a report text. ● Children's written responses on the photocopiable sheet and oral responses.	**Reading AF2** ● Some specific, straightforward information recalled. ● Generally clear idea of where to look for information. **Writing AF3** ● Some basic sequencing of ideas or material. ● Openings and/or closings sometimes signalled.	**Reading AF2** ● Simple, most obvious points identified though there may also be some misunderstanding. ● Some comments include quotations from or references to text, but not always relevant. **Writing AF3** ● Some attempt to organise ideas with related points placed next to each other. ● Openings and closings usually signalled. ● Some attempt to sequence ideas or material logically.	I can use a graphic organiser.
Phase ③ activities pages 103–104				
Finding out Children can recognise the structure and language features of a non-chronological report.	● Paired activity where children use information on a photocopiable to complete an interactive activity. ● Children's completed interactive activity and oral responses.	**Reading AF4** ● Some awareness of use of features of organisation.	**Reading AF4** ● A few basic features of organisation at text level identified, with little or no linked comment.	I can locate information within a contents page or index.
Captions and labels Children can recognise the structure and language features of a non-chronological report.	● Supported activity where children add labels and captions to an illustration. ● Children's completed interactive activity and oral responses.	**Reading AF5** ● Some effective language choices noted. ● Some familiar patterns of language identified.	**Reading AF5** ● A few basic features of writer's use of language identified, but with little or no comment.	I can use captions and labels correctly.

Unit 1 📖 Reports

NON-FICTION

Learning outcomes	Assessment opportunity and evidence	Assessment focuses (AFs)		Success criteria
		Level 2	Level 3	
Phase ④ activity page 105				
Writing a non-chronological report Children can note information collected from reading more than one source and present it in the form of a non-chronological report.	• Supported group activity where children research information and present it in a writing frame. • Children's oral and written responses and paired evaluations.	**Writing AF3** • Some basic sequencing of ideas or material. • Openings and/or closings sometimes signalled.	**Writing AF3** • Some attempt to organise ideas with related points placed next to each other. • Openings and closings usually signalled. • Some attempt to sequence ideas or material logically.	• I can use a writing frame to present a non-chronological report. • I can use headings and subheadings. • I can research information.

Learning outcomes	Assessment opportunity and evidence	Assessment focuses (AFs)		Success criteria
		Level 4	Level 5	
Phase ① activities pages 101–103				
Key points Children demonstrate that they have understood information read from a book or screen by noting the main points.	• Paired activity where children highlight key words in report text. • Children's completed interactive activity and teacher's notes.	**Reading AF2** • Some relevant points identified. • Comments supported by some generally relevant textual reference or quotation.	**Reading AF2** • Most relevant points clearly identified, including those selected from different places in the text. • Comments generally supported by relevant textual reference or quotation, even when points made are not always accurate.	I can identify key ideas in paragraphs.
Key facts Children demonstrate that they have understood information read from a book or screen by noting the main points.	• Paired activity where children highlight key facts in report text. • Children's written responses and teacher's notes.	**Reading AF2** • Some relevant points identified. • Comments supported by some generally relevant textual reference or quotation.	**Reading AF2** • Most relevant points clearly identified, including those selected from different places in the text. • Comments generally supported by relevant textual reference or quotation, even when points made are not always accurate.	I can identify key facts.
Report plan Children demonstrate that they have understood information read from a book or screen by noting the main points.	• Independent activity where children make notes on a graphic organiser for a report text. • Children's written responses on the photocopiable sheet and oral responses.	**Reading AF2** • Some relevant points identified. • Comments supported by some generally relevant textual reference or quotation. **Writing AF3** • Ideas organised by clustering related points or by time sequence • Ideas are organised simply with a fitting opening and closing, sometimes linked. • Ideas or material generally in logical sequence but overall direction of writing not always clearly signalled.	**Reading AF2** • Most relevant points clearly identified, including those selected from different places in the text. • Comments generally supported by relevant textual reference or quotation, even when points made are not always accurate. **Writing AF3** • Material is structured clearly, with sentences organised into appropriate paragraphs. • Development of material is effectively managed across text. • Overall direction of the text supported by clear links between paragraphs.	I can use a graphic organiser.

Unit 1 🗂 Reports

Learning outcomes	Assessment opportunity and evidence	Assessment focuses (AFs)		Success criteria
		Level 4	Level 5	
Phase ③ activities pages 103-104				
Finding out Children can recognise the structure and language features of a non-chronological report.	• Paired activity where children use information on a photocopiable to complete an interactive activity. • Children's completed interactive activity and oral responses.	**Reading AF4** • Some structural choices identified with simple comment. • Some basic features of organisation at text level identified.	**Reading AF4** • Comments on structural choices show some general awareness of writer's craft. • Various features relating to organisation at text level, including form, are clearly identified, with some explanation.	I can locate information within a contents page or index.
Captions and labels Children can recognise the structure and language features of a non-chronological report.	• Independent activity where children add labels and captions to an illustration. • Children's completed interactive activity and oral responses.	**Reading AF5** • Some basic features of writer's use of language identified. • Simple comments on writer's choices.	**Reading AF5** • Various features of writer's use of language identified, with some explanation. • Comments show some awareness of the effect of writer's language choices.	I can use captions and labels correctly.
Phase ④ activity page 105				
Writing a non-chronological report Children can note information collected from reading more than one source and present it in the form of a non-chronological report.	• Independent activity where children research information and present it in a writing frame. • Children's oral and written responses and paired evaluations.	**Writing AF3** • Ideas organised by clustering related points or by time sequence. • Ideas are organised simply with a fitting opening and closing, sometimes linked. • Ideas or material generally in logical sequence but overall direction of writing not always clearly signalled.	**Writing AF3** • Material is structured clearly, with sentences organised into appropriate paragraphs. • Development of material is effectively managed across text. • Overall direction of the text supported by clear links between paragraphs.	• I can use a writing frame to present a non-chronological report. • I can use headings and subheadings. • I can research information.

Phase ① Key points

Learning outcome
Children demonstrate that they have understood information read from a book or screen by noting the main points.

Success criteria
I can identify key ideas in paragraphs.

Setting the context
The children should have explored the difference between fiction and non-fiction and have understood the purpose and language features of a report. They should have read various reports and identified key words and ideas. Invite children working at levels 4–5 to independently identify the key points of the report in the interactive activity 'Key points'. Children working at levels 2–3, work in pairs supported by an adult.

Assessment opportunity
Children working at levels 2–3 work in a supported group to discuss the text before highlighting the key words. When the children have completed each screen, an adult can ask them to give reasons for their choices and can make notes of reasons. Children working at levels 4–5 work on the same task independently.

Assessment evidence
At levels 2–3, children will identify the simplest and most obvious points, though they may make the occasional error. At levels 4–5 they will be more secure in identifying the key points, even if they come from different places in the text, and will be able to support what they say with specific references. Use the completed activity and observational notes to provide evidence towards Reading AF2.

Next steps:
Support: Discuss each paragraph on the screen and eliminate what cannot be the key point.
Extension: Ask children to write a heading for each screen and a subheading for each paragraph.

Key aspects of learning
Information processing: Children will identify relevant information from a range of sources on paper and on screen.
Social skills: When working collaboratively, children will listen to and respect other people's ideas.
Communication: Children will develop their ability to discuss the content and presentation of the reports they are listening to, reading and writing. They will often work collaboratively in pairs and groups. They will communicate outcomes orally, in writing and through ICT.

Phase ① Key facts

Learning outcome
Children demonstrate that they have understood information read from a book or screen by noting the main points.

Success criteria
I can identify key facts.

Setting the context
The children should have explored the difference between fiction and non-fiction texts and have understood the purpose and language features of a report. They should have read reports and identified key words and ideas in paragraphs. They will have summarised reports by identifying the key facts. Invite the children to work on the photocopiable page 'Key facts' (version 1 or 2) and highlight the key facts that would be used in a summary of the text. Children working at levels 4–5 can use version 2 of the photocopiable page, and those at levels 2–3 can work on version 1.

Assessment opportunity

Children working at levels 2–3 work in pairs in a group to discuss the text with the supporting adult before highlighting the key facts. The adult can assist them in identifying the main facts by asking questions, for example: *Do you think the clause 'there are no dinosaurs alive' is a key fact?* (No, because everyone knows that.) *Do you think the numbers that describe time are key facts?* (Yes, they are important information.) Children working at levels 4–5 will work in pairs on the same task.

Assessment evidence

At levels 2–3, children will identify many of the key facts, though they may sometimes be sidetracked by obvious statements that give little or no information (such as the opening phrase). At levels 4–5, children will be more secure in identifying the key facts, even if they come from different places in the text, and will be able to support what they say with specific references. This activity will provide evidence towards Reading AF2.

Next steps

Support: Ask children to highlight one key fact only in each paragraph.
Extension: Ask children to write a summary of the text using their key facts.

Key aspects of learning

Information processing: Children will identify relevant information from a range of sources on paper and on screen.
Social skills: When working collaboratively, children will listen to and respect other people's ideas.
Communication: Children will develop their ability to discuss the content and presentation of the reports they are listening to, reading and writing. They will often work collaboratively in pairs and groups. They will communicate outcomes orally, in writing and through ICT.

Phase ① Report plan

Learning outcome
Children demonstrate that they have understood information read from a book or screen by noting the main points.

Success criteria

I can use a graphic organiser.

Setting the context

This activity should be carried out once the children have explored the difference between fiction and non-fiction texts and have understood the purpose and language features of report text. They should have identified key facts about a topic and have summarised report texts in writing. Run this activity when the children have used graphic organisers. Invite them to use their key facts from text on the photocopiable page 'Key facts' (version 1 or 2) and write them in the graphic organiser on the photocopiable page 'Report plan' (version 1 or 2). Provide children working at levels 2–3 with version 1 and those at levels 4–5 with version 2 of each photocopiable page. Provide the children with other books about dinosaurs so they can add extra information to the organiser in at least one of the empty frames.

Assessment opportunity

Children working at levels 2–3 work in a supported group and discuss which key facts to include. An adult can assist them in deciding on one new subheading to add and the sort of facts to include there, for example: *What information does the photocopiable page 'Key facts' not give?* (It does not tell us about what dinosaurs ate.) *Would that be good information for a report about dinosaurs?* Children working at levels 4–5 will work independently.

Assessment evidence

At levels 2–3, children will be dependent on the key facts from the previous activity and may find it difficult to come up with subheadings. They will order their material logically and will signal the information needed for opening and closing the text. At levels 4–5, children will produce well-structured plans, with related points (including those they have added) clustered together and the overall direction of the text clearly indicated. Use children's written responses and your notes to provide evidence towards Reading AF2 and Writing AF3.

Next steps
Support: Remind children to use the index and contents list in books.
Extension: Invite children to make notes in all the empty frames.

Key aspects of learning
Information processing: Children will identify relevant information from a range of sources on paper and on screen and use this to write their own non-chronological reports.
Social skills: When working collaboratively, children will listen to and respect other people's ideas.
Communication: Children will develop their ability to discuss the content and presentation of the reports they are listening to, reading and writing. They will often work collaboratively in pairs and groups. They will communicate outcomes orally, in writing and through ICT.

Phase ③ Finding out

Learning outcome
Children can recognise the structure and language features of a non-chronological report.

Success criteria
I can locate information within a contents page or index.

Setting the context
The children should have used contents pages and indexes to research and answer questions. Ensure the children know where to find the contents page and the index in a book. Provide them with copies of the photocopiable page 'Finding out'. Discuss what the page contains, such as a contents page and an index for a non-fiction book on the topic of light. Explain that they are to use the information on this page to answer a series of true or false questions in the interactive activity 'Finding out'.

Assessment opportunity
Children working at all levels work with a partner and discuss the questions asked in the interactive activity, using the photocopiable page 'Finding out' to cross-check their answers. The children check their results as they complete each screen. Discuss the results with individuals and ask them to say which aspects of using a contents page and an index they feel secure about and which aspects need more learning. Make notes on the children's abilities to evaluate their own work.

Assessment evidence
At levels 2–3, children will have a basic awareness of the features of contents pages and indexes. At levels 4–5, children will be more aware of ways in which they can put these features to good use when consulting reference books. They will therefore be more successful in answering the questions correctly. Use the activity results and your comments to provide evidence for Reading AF4.

Next steps
Support: Send non-fiction report books home over a period of several days with a different question each time for the children to research using the index.
Extension: Challenge groups to find answer to questions in the shortest time.

Key aspects of learning
Information processing: Children will identify relevant information from a range of sources on paper and on screen.
Evaluation: Children will present information orally and in writing. They will discuss success criteria, give feedback to others and judge the effectiveness of their own work.

Social skills: When working collaboratively, children will listen to and respect other people's ideas.

Communication: Children will develop their ability to discuss the content and presentation of the reports they are listening to, reading and writing. They will often work collaboratively in pairs and groups. They will communicate outcomes orally, in writing and through ICT.

Phase ③ Captions and labels

Learning outcome
Children can recognise the structure and language features of a non-chronological report.

Success criteria
I can use captions and labels correctly.

Setting the context
The children should have explored the purpose of captions and labels in non-fiction texts. Ensure they know the difference between captions and labels. Explain that they are going to see an illustration on the interactive activity 'Captions and labels' with spaces for labels or captions. Tell them to drag and drop the correct label or caption into the correct space on the screen.

Assessment opportunity
A supporting adult can observe those working at levels 2-3 and ask them to explain the reasons for their choices, making notes. Ask individual children to explain what the purpose of a caption is and the purpose of a label. Make notes of their responses. Children working at levels 4-5 work independently.

Assessment evidence
At levels 2-3, children will allocate correctly those items that show the most obvious caption or label features, but may have difficulty with those needing more subtle judgment. At levels 4-5, children will be more able to recognise key language features, which will give them clues to the text type of each item. Use the activity to provide evidence for Reading AF5.

Next steps
Support: Mask the labels and captions on illustrations in non-fiction texts and ask children to write the label or caption they think should be used.
Extension: Invite children to revisit report texts they have written, swap with a partner and draw and label an illustration that is appropriate to the text.

Key aspects of learning
Information processing: Children will identify relevant information from a range of sources on paper and on screen and use this to write their own non-chronological reports.
Communication: Children will develop their ability to discuss the content and presentation of the reports they are listening to, reading and writing. They will often work collaboratively in pairs and groups. They will communicate outcomes orally, in writing and through ICT.

NON-FICTION

Phase ④ Writing a non-chronological report

Learning outcome
Children can note information collected from reading more than one source and present it in the form of a non-chronological report.

Success criteria
- I can use a writing frame to present a non-chronological report.
- I can use headings and subheadings.
- I can research information.

Setting the context
The children should have explored the features of non-chronological reports. Provide a selection of books on a similar topic for the children to refer to during this activity. Explain that they are going to plan a non-chronological report on the topic and write their main ideas and key pieces of information on a report writing frame.

Assessment opportunity
Children working at levels 2–3 work in small groups, using the photocopiable page 'Non-chronological report' (version 1). A supporting adult can question them to draw out their ideas and explain their choices of facts and organisation. They then complete notes for two subheadings rather than three. Those working at levels 4–5 work independently to complete notes on the photocopiable page 'Non-chronological report' (version 2). You could ask the children to swap sheets to evaluate one another's work. Make notes of the children's responses.

Assessment evidence
At levels 2–3, children will sequence their ideas logically and will include suggestions for opening and closing the report. At levels 4–5, children will show a more secure mastery of the form, with the overall direction of the report clearly signalled between paragraphs. The opening and closing paragraphs may be linked in some way, and there may be other echoes between sections, showing a clear development of the content throughout. Use the children's completed writing frames to provide evidence towards Writing AF3.

Next steps
Support: Invite children to use their notes to write the introduction and one more paragraph in full.
Extension: Invite children to use their notes to write their report text in full.

Key aspects of learning
Enquiry: Children will ask questions arising from work in another area of the curriculum (for example, teeth and eating), research and then plan how to present the information effectively.
Information processing: Children will identify relevant information from a range of sources on paper and on screen and use this to write their own non-chronological reports.
Evaluation: Children will present information orally and in writing. They will discuss success criteria, give feedback to others and judge the effectiveness of their own work.
Communication: Children will develop their ability to discuss the content and presentation of the reports they are listening to, reading and writing. They will often work collaboratively in pairs and groups. They will communicate outcomes orally, in writing and through ICT.

Periodic assessment

Reading

Learning outcome
Children can recognise the structure and language features of a non-chronological report.

Success criteria
● I can understand the difference between fiction and non-fiction text types.
● I can recognise the difference between an index and the contents page.
● I can recognise the difference between non-chronological reports and other text types.

Setting the context
This assessment should be undertaken once the children have completed Non-fiction Unit 1 and have become familiar with the typical language (present-tense verbs), layout (headings, subheadings, paragraphs) and the use of illustrations with labels and captions. Discuss individual children's achievements with them. Ask them to suggest what they found difficult about the work in the unit and what they found easy and compare their responses with the comments made on the class list. Invite the children to complete the interactive activity 'Non-fiction 1 Reading assessment'.

Assessment opportunity
This activity provides an opportunity for the children to demonstrate their understanding of the way in which report text differs from other types of text. Invite the children to complete the interactive activity independently. They choose the correct answers for five different screens and check their answers interactively.

Assessment evidence
Use the children's completed activities and oral comments to provide evidence towards Reading AF4. At levels 2–3, children will successfully identify most of the basic text features but will find it difficult to comment on them. At levels 4–5, children will show greater awareness of the writer's craft and will better understand the functions of the features. They will be able to comment on the text with remarks showing an understanding of why the author has approached a particular detail in a certain way, and why it is in its current position. Use this activity as well as examples of children's work throughout this unit to make overall level judgements for Reading.

Periodic assessment

Writing

Learning outcome
Children note information from reading more than one source and present it in the form of a non-chronological report.

Success criteria
- I can locate information.
- I can write a paragraph.
- I can use captions and labels correctly.
- I can use headings and subheadings.

Setting the context
This assessment should be carried out once the children have completed Non-fiction Unit 1. Collect the work that has been completed during the course of the unit and discuss individual children's achievements with them. Ask them to suggest what they found difficult about the work in the unit and what they found easy. Refer them to the work they did in using a graphic organiser and a writing frame. Invite them to use the notes from either or both of these pages to write a non-chronological report.

Assessment opportunity
Children working at levels 2-3, work in a group to write an introduction, two paragraphs and a concluding statement. When their texts are complete, invite the groups to report on how they worked together and describe each other's contributions to the group task. Working in small groups, invite the children working at levels 4-5 to write an introduction to the topic, add three or more paragraphs about it and a conclusion. They should share the work between them and collaborate to complete a full non-chronological report. Make notes on their responses.

Assessment evidence
Use the children's completed reports and your notes to provide evidence towards all the Writing AFs, especially AF3. At levels 2-3, children will sequence their ideas logically and include suggestions for opening and closing the report. They will use simple vocabulary and sentence structure, and may overuse the most common connectives. At levels 4-5, children will combine a more varied writing style with secure mastery of the form, with the overall direction of the report clearly signalled. The opening and closing paragraphs may be linked and other echoes between sections will show a clear development of the content throughout. Use this activity as well as examples of children's work throughout this unit to make overall level judgements for Writing.

Name _____   Date _____

Key facts (1)

◼ Highlight or underline the key facts in each paragraph.

There was a time when dinosaurs roamed the earth and were the main species on the planet. There were many different types of dinosaur and they were all sorts of shapes and sizes. The most fierce dinosaur was Tyrannosaurus Rex. It was about 12 metres long and six metres tall. Other dinosaurs were very small; Composagnathus is the smallest dinosaur that has so far been discovered and was about the same size as a chicken.

Other reptiles which were related to dinosaurs flew. Many scientists think they were the distant ancestors of modern birds. Some dinosaurs could swim but none of them actually lived in water. However, there were other reptiles at the time of the dinosaurs that lived in water.

The last dinosaurs died out 65 million years ago. No one knows for certain why the dinosaur age came to an end. The most accepted cause is that an asteroid hit the earth and caused a great change in climate. The dinosaurs could not adapt to the changes and so became extinct.

Illustration © 2009, Anna Godwin.

Red
Amber
Green

I can identify key facts. ◻

Name   Date

Report plan (1)

■ Make notes for a report on dinosaurs. Add other subheadings in the empty frames.

Main heading **Dinosaurs**		
Introduction	Appearances	Habitats
Food		

I can use a graphic organiser. ⬜

Red ⬤ Amber ⬤ Green ⬤

NON-FICTION

NON-FICTION
UNIT 2 Instructions

Literacy objectives

Speak and listen for a wide range of purposes in different contexts
Strand 1 Speaking
- Explain process or present information, ensuring that items are clearly sequenced, relevant details are included and accounts are ended effectively.

Strand 3 Group discussion and interaction
- Use talk to organise roles and action.
- Actively include and respond to all members of the group.

Read and write for a range of purposes on paper and on screen
Strand 6 Word structure and spelling
- Spell unfamiliar words using known conventions including grapheme–phoneme correspondence and morphological rules.

Strand 7 Understanding and interpreting texts
- Identify how different texts are organised, including reference texts, magazines and leaflets, on paper and on screen.

Strand 9 Creating and shaping texts
- Make decisions about form and purpose, identify success criteria and use them to evaluate their writing.
- Select and use a range of technical and descriptive vocabulary.
- Use layout, format, graphics and illustrations for different purposes.

Strand 10 Text structure and organisation
- Signal sequence, place and time to give coherence.
- Group related material into paragraphs.

Strand 11 Sentence structure and punctuation
- Show relationships of time, reason and cause through subordination and connectives.
- Compose sentences using adjectives, verbs and nouns for precision, clarity and impact.

Strand 12 Presentation
- Write with consistency in the size and proportion of letters and spacing within and between words, using the correct formation of handwriting joins.
- Develop accuracy and speed when using keyboard skills to type, edit and re-draft.

Key aspects of learning

Information processing
● Children will process information from a range of media and use the information for their own instructional sequences.
Social skills
● When orally rehearsing instructions, children will learn about relating to group members effectively.
Communication
● Children will often work collaboratively in paired, group and whole-class contexts. They will communicate outcomes orally, in writing and through ICT if appropriate.
Reasoning
● Children will explain their opinion about the effectiveness of instructional texts against agreed success criteria.
Evaluation
● Children will have regular opportunities to watch others' oral rehearsals and use these to improve their sequencing and use of imperative vocabulary.

Assessment focuses

Reading
AF4 (*identify and comment on the structure and organisation of texts, including grammatical and presentational features at text level*).

Writing
AF2 (*produce texts which are appropriate to task, reader and purpose*).
AF3 (*organise and present whole texts effectively, sequencing and structuring information, ideas and events*).
AF5 (*vary sentences for clarity, purpose and effect*).

Speaking and listening
Speaking (speak with clarity, intonation and pace).
Group discussion and interaction (support others, take turns).

Resources

Phase 1
Photocopiable page, 'Features of instructions' (versions 1 and 2)
Interactive activity, 'Sequencing instructions'
Phase 2
Photocopiable page, 'Instructions' (versions 1 and 2)
Phase 3
Interactive activity, 'Polished instructions'
Periodic assessment
Interactive activity, 'Non-fiction 2 Reading assessment'
Photocopiable page 'Non-fiction 2 Writing assessment'

Unit 2 ⬜ Instructions

Learning outcomes	Assessment opportunity and evidence	Assessment focuses (AFs)		Success criteria
		Level 2	Level 3	
Phase ① activity page 114				
Features of Instructions • Children can recognise the structure and language features of instructional text. • Children can express a view clearly as part of a class or group discussion.	• Supported group activity where children annotate the features of a set of instructions. • Children's written and oral responses and teacher's notes.	**Reading AF4** • Some awareness of use of features of organisation.	**Reading AF4** • A few basic features of organisation at text level identified, with little or no linked comment.	I can identify features of an instructional text.
Phase ② activity page 115				
Planning a set of instructions Children can orally produce instructions, evaluate their effectiveness and develop them into a chronological sequence.	• Supported group activity where children rehearse a set of instructions, write a draft and present their instructions orally. • Children's own evaluations, oral presentations and written responses.	**Writing AF2** • Some basic purpose established. • Some appropriate features of the given form used. • Some attempts to adopt appropriate style.	**Writing AF2** • Purpose established at a general level. • Main features of selected form sometimes signalled to the reader. • Some attempts at appropriate style, with attention to reader.	• I can plan oral instructions. • I can rehearse oral instructions. • I can write a draft a set of instructions.
Phase ③ activity page 116				
Polished instructions Children can write an instructional text using selective adverbial language, sequenced imperative statements and presentational features such as bullet points or numbering.	• Paired and independent activity where children choose adverbs for instructions in an interactive activity and re-write their draft instructions in a polished form. • Children's oral responses to the interactive activity and their written responses.	**Writing AF3** • Some basic sequencing of ideas or material. • Openings and/or closings sometimes signalled. **Writing AF5** • Some variation in sentence openings. • Mainly simple sentences with *and* used to connect clauses. • Past and present tense generally consistent.	**Writing AF3** • Some attempt to organise ideas with related points placed next to each other. • Openings and closings usually signalled. • Some attempt to sequence ideas or material logically. **Writing AF5** • Reliance mainly on simply structured sentences, variation with support. • *and, but, so* are the most common connectives, subordination occasionally. • Some limited variation in use of tense and verb forms, not always secure.	• I can plan a recipe. • I can polish notes.

Unit 2 ◻ Instructions

Learning outcomes	Assessment opportunity and evidence	Assessment focuses (AFs)		Success criteria
		Level 4	Level 5	
Phase ① activity page 114				
Features of instructions • Children can recognise the structure and language features of instructional text. • Children can express a view clearly as part of a class or group discussion.	• Independent group activity where children annotate the features of a set of instructions. • Children's written and oral responses.	**Reading AF4** • Some structural choices identified with simple comment. • Some basic features of organisation at text level identified.	**Reading AF4** • Comments on structural choices show some general awareness of writer's craft. • Various features relating to organisation at text level, including form, are clearly identified, with some explanation.	I can identify features of an instructional text.
Phase ② activity page 115				
Planning a set of instructions Children can orally produce instructions, evaluate their effectiveness and develop them into a chronological sequence.	• Paired activity where children rehearse a set of instructions, write a draft and present their instructions orally. • Children's own evaluations, oral presentations and written responses.	**Writing AF2** • Main purpose of writing is clear but not always consistently maintained. • Main features of selected form are clear and appropriate to purpose. • Style generally appropriate to task, though awareness of reader not always sustained.	**Writing AF2** • Main purpose of writing is clear and consistently maintained. • Features of selected form clearly established with some adaptation to purpose. • Appropriate style clearly established to maintain reader's interest throughout.	• I can plan oral instructions. • I can rehearse oral instructions. • I can write a draft a set of instructions.
Phase ③ activity page 116				
Polished instructions Children can write an instructional text using selective adverbial language, sequenced imperative statements and presentational features such as bullet points or numbering.	• Paired and independent activity where children choose adverbs for instructions in an interactive activity and re-write their draft instructions in a polished form. • Children's oral responses to the interactive activity and their written responses.	**Writing AF3** • Ideas organised by clustering related points or by time sequence. • Ideas are organised simply with a fitting opening and closing, sometimes linked. • Ideas or material generally in logical sequence but overall direction of writing not always clearly signalled. **Writing AF5** • Some variety in length, structure or subject of sentences. • Use of some subordinating connectives throughout the text. • Some variation, generally accurate, in tense and verb forms.	**Writing AF3** • Material is structured clearly, with sentences organised into appropriate paragraphs. • Development of material is effectively managed across text. • Overall direction of the text supported by clear links between paragraphs. **Writing AF5** • A variety of sentence lengths, structures and subjects provides clarity and emphasis. • Wider range of connectives used to clarify relationship between ideas. • Some features of sentence structure used to build up detail or convey shades of meaning.	• I can plan a recipe. • I can polish notes.

NON-FICTION

Phase ① Features of instructions

Learning outcomes
- Children can recognise the structure and language features of instructional text.
- Children can express a view clearly as part of a class or group discussion.

Success criteria
I can identify features of an instructional text.

Setting the context
This activity should be carried out after the children have explored the purpose and language features of instructional text through shared, guided and independent reading. They should have read instructional text both in print and on screen, and watched an instructional programme, for example, a cookery programme. They should have had opportunities to explore and identify key language and layout features. Invite children working at levels 4-5 to annotate the photocopiable page 'Features of instructions' (version 2) independently. Children working at levels 2-3 work in a small group supported by an adult, using version 1 of the photocopiable page.

Assessment opportunity
Children working at levels 2-3 work in a supported group and discuss the text as a group before annotating the page independently. The adult asks the children to find features by posing questions such as, *How does the text indicate the aim? What is the purpose of the bulleted list? Why are numbers used? Where is the verb in most of the sentences?* and so on. The supporting adult makes notes of the children's responses. Children working at levels 4-5 work in independent groups and discuss the features and effectiveness of the text. They then annotate the text independently.

Assessment evidence
At levels 2-3, children will successfully identify most of the basic text features but will find it difficult to comment on them. At levels 4-5, children will show greater awareness of the writer's craft and will better understand the functions of the features. They will be able to comment on the text with remarks showing an understanding of why the author has approached a particular detail in a certain way, and why it is in its current position. Use the children's written responses, oral feedback and notes made during the levels 2-3 discussions to provide evidence for Reading AF4.

Next steps
Support: Children who need extra practice perform the interactive sequencing activity 'Sequencing instructions'.
Extension: Ask the children to practise giving a set of oral instructions to a partner using the typical language features of instructional text.

Key aspects of learning
Information processing: Children will process information from a range of media and use the information for their own instructional sequences.
Social skills: When orally rehearsing instructions, children will learn about relating to group members effectively.
Communication: Children will often work collaboratively in paired, group and whole-class contexts. They will communicate outcomes orally, in writing and through ICT if appropriate.

Phase ② Planning a set of instructions

Learning outcome
Children can orally produce instructions, evaluate their effectiveness and develop them into a chronological sequence.

Success criteria
- I can plan oral instructions.
- I can rehearse oral instructions.
- I can write a draft set of instructions.

Setting the context
This activity should be carried out after the children have explored the language and layout of written instructions and have had practice at giving a set of oral instructions. Invite the children to work with a partner and discuss how to create a set of instructions on a specific topic, for example, making a fruit salad. Ask them to work out the language and sequence orally and rehearse it in pairs. Provide the pairs of children with copies of photocopiable page 'Instructions' (version 1 for children working at levels 2-3 and version 2 for levels 4-5 children) and ask them to collaborate to write a draft of their rehearsed instructions.

Assessment opportunity
Children working at levels 2-3 work in pairs in a supported group. The supporting adult can assist them in identifying the main elements, for example: *What do you need to make a fruit salad? In what order should you say these items? What sorts of words can you use to describe the sequence?* When the children have rehearsed and written a draft set of instructions, invite them in pairs to present their instructions orally, for the group or class, and invite others to comment on their effectiveness. Children working at levels 4-5 work independently in pairs. Make notes on the children's responses.

Assessment evidence
At levels 2-3, children will produce a plan that is fit for purpose and includes the main features required. At levels 4-5, children will produce a plan without being prompted on what to include. If the particular instructions that they are writing require some variation to the standard plan, they will be able to adapt it accordingly. Use the children's oral presentations and written drafts, together with notes made during the discussions and rehearsals, to provide evidence towards Writing AF2.

Next steps
Support: Cut a set of instructions into strips and let those children who struggled to write or perform an effective sequence practise re-ordering them.
Extension: Children write their instructions using a computer and add graphics as appropriate.

Key aspects of learning
Information processing: Children will process information from a range of media and use the information for their own instructional sequences.
Reasoning: Children will explain their opinion about the effectiveness of instructional texts against agreed success criteria.
Evaluation: Children will have regular opportunities to watch others' oral rehearsals and use these to improve their sequencing and use of imperative vocabulary.
Social skills: When orally rehearsing instructions, children will learn about relating to group members effectively.
Communication: Children will work collaboratively in paired, group and whole-class contexts. They will communicate outcomes orally, in writing and through ICT if appropriate.

NON-FICTION

Phase ③ Polished instructions

Learning outcome
Children can write an instructional text using selective adverbial language, sequenced imperative statements and presentational features such as bullet points or numbering.

Success criteria
● I can plan a recipe.
● I can polish notes.

Setting the context
This activity should be carried out after the children have explored language and layout of instructional text through shared, guided and independent reading. They should have rehearsed oral presentations of instructions, written drafts and performed them for others. Invite the children to use their draft recipes, written in the previous assessment activity, 'Planning a set of instructions', and write them up as a polished set of notes. Ensure the children understand how to make use of adverbial language in instructions by asking them to complete the interactive activity 'Polished instructions', before rewriting their draft notes.

Assessment opportunity
The children work in pairs to do the interactive activity and discuss the effect of using different adverbs in each of the sentences. Ask for feedback about their choices and make notes on the class list. The children then independently write their draft instructions as a polished sequence.

Assessment evidence
At levels 2–3, children will correctly position different elements of the text. The instruction narrative may be repetitive, with little variation in sentence structure, and the children may lack confidence in using adverbs. At levels 4–5, children will give clear, step-by-step instructions at each stage. They will be able to predict how different adverbs might affect what the reader does – and this will put them at an advantage in writing instructions that may be used successfully. Use the children's written responses to provide evidence for Writing AF3. Notes made on feedback from the interactive activity provide evidence for Writing AF5.

Next steps
Support: Create a splat board or word wall for those children who struggle to choose appropriate adverbs, and ask them to add adverbs they encounter when reading different types of instruction text.
Extension: Invite children to create a PowerPoint® presentation of their instructions.

Key aspects of learning
Information processing: Children will process information from a range of media and use the information for their own instructional sequences.
Reasoning: Children will explain their opinion about the effectiveness of instructional texts against agreed success criteria.
Evaluation: Children will have regular opportunities to watch others' oral rehearsals and use these to improve their sequencing and use of imperative vocabulary.
Social skills: When orally rehearsing instructions, children will learn about relating to group members effectively.
Communication: Children will work collaboratively in paired, group and whole-class contexts. They will communicate outcomes orally, in writing and through ICT if appropriate.

Periodic assessment

Reading

Learning outcome
Children can recognise the structure and language features of instructional text.

Success criteria
I can identify features of instructional text.

Setting the context
This assessment should be undertaken after the children have completed Non-fiction Unit 2 and have become familiar with the typical language (imperative verbs, factual adjectives, specific details) and layout (clear sequence). Invite children to complete the interactive activity 'Non-fiction 2 Reading assessment' to show their understanding of the way instructional text differs from other types of text.

Assessment opportunity
Invite the children to complete the interactive activity independently. They will choose the answers for three different screens and check their answers.

Assessment evidence
Use the children's completed activities and your notes to provide evidence for Reading AF4. At levels 2–3, children will identify and understand the basic features of an instructional text, and will know how these are organised. At levels 4–5, children will show a more general awareness of the writer's craft and a clearer understanding of why particular structural decisions have been made.

Writing

Learning outcome
Children can write an instructional text using selective adverbial language, sequenced imperative statements and presentational features such as bullet points and numbering.

Success criteria
I can write and evaluate instructions.

Setting the context
This assessment should be carried out after the children have completed Non-fiction Unit 2. Invite the children to work with a partner. Tell them to swap their polished set of written instructions, and read and evaluate each other's writing. Children working at levels 2–3 can work with a supporting adult to read and evaluate their partner's writing. Provide all the children with a copy of the photocopiable page 'Non-fiction 2 Writing assessment' to refer to.

Assessment opportunity
This activity provides an opportunity for children to peer-assess each other's instruction writing against a set of success criteria. When they have read and examined each other's writing using the prompts on the photocopiable page, invite the children to give oral feedback about each other's instructions.

Assessment evidence
Use the children's instruction texts, their written evaluations and notes made on their oral feedback to provide evidence for Writing AF2 and AF3. At levels 2–3, children will correctly position different elements of the text. The instruction narrative may be repetitive but the text will generally be fit for purpose. At levels 4–5, children will give clear, step-by-step instructions at each stage. The main purpose of the text will be clearly and consistently maintained and the writing style will be appropriate to the task.

NON-FICTION

Name   Date

Features of instructions (1)

■ Mark up the typical features and language used in this set of instructions. Use words and phrases from the box below to help you.

How to polish shoes

What you need:

- a sheet of newspaper
- a tin of shoe polish
- 2 brushes
- I duster

What you do:

1. First remove any mud or dust from each shoe.
2. Place the newspaper on the floor or on a table.
3. Place the shoes on the newspaper.
4. Dip one of the brushes into the tin of polish. Do not overload the brush.
5. Coat one shoe with polish, rubbing it into the surface thoroughly.
6. Repeat with the next shoe.
7. Allow 5 minutes for the shoes to absorb the polish.
8. Using the other brush, brush the shoes.
9. Take the duster and rub the shoes to remove any remaining polish and shine the shoes.
10. Clear away the paper, brushes and polish when you have finished.
11. Finally, wash your hands.

The result will be clean and shiny shoes.

> - title tells you the purpose   • clear sequence of steps   • outcome
> - numbered steps   • bullet-pointed list   • time-based connectives
> - command verbs at the beginning of sentences
> - what is needed listed in the order you need them

Illustration © 2009 Anna Godwin

Red
Amber   I can identify features of an instructional text.
Green

Name	Date

Instructions (1)

Aim:

What is needed (list everything):

What to do (sequence of steps; use numbers or bullets; use time connectives; use command verbs):

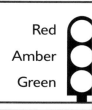

Red I can plan oral instructions. ☐

Amber I can rehearse oral instructions. ☐

Green I can write a draft set of instructions. ☐

NON-FICTION

UNIT 3 Information texts

Literacy objectives

Speak and listen for a wide range of purposes in different contexts

Strand 1 Speaking
- Explain process or present information, ensuring that items are clearly sequenced, relevant details are included and accounts are ended effectively.

Strand 3 Group discussion and interaction
- Use talk to organise roles and action.
- Actively include and respond to all members of the group.

Read and write for a range of purposes on paper and on screen

Strand 7 Understanding and interpreting texts
- Identify how different texts are organised, including reference texts, magazines and leaflets, on paper and on screen.

Strand 8 Engaging with and responding to texts
- Identify features that writers use to provoke readers' reactions.

Strand 9 Creating and shaping texts
- Make decisions about form and purpose, identify success criteria and use them to evaluate their writing.
- Write non-narrative texts using structures of different text types.
- Select and use a range of technical and descriptive vocabulary.
- Use layout, format, graphics and illustrations for different purposes.

Strand 10 Text structure and organisation
- Signal sequence, place and time to give coherence.
- Group related material into paragraphs.

Strand 11 Sentence structure and punctuation
- Show relationships of time, reason and cause through subordination and connectives.
- Compose sentences using adjectives, verbs and nouns for precision, clarity and impact.

Key aspects of learning

Enquiry
- Children will ask questions, research and then plan how to present the information effectively.

Information processing
- Children will identify relevant information from a range of sources on paper and on screen.

Communication
- Children will often work collaboratively in paired, group and whole-class contexts. They will communicate outcomes orally, in writing and through ICT if appropriate.

Reasoning
- Children will explain their opinion about the effectiveness of simple persuasive texts against agreed success criteria.

Social skills
- When developing collaborative writing, children will learn to listen to and respect others' viewpoints and take on different roles within a group to complete a task.

Assessment focuses

Reading
AF2 *(understand, describe, select or retrieve information, events or ideas from texts and use quotation and reference to text).*
AF4 *(identify and comment on the structure and organisation of texts, including grammatical and presentational features at text level).*
AF6 *(identify and comment on writers' purposes and viewpoints and the overall effect of the text on the reader).*

Writing
AF5 *(vary sentences for clarity, purpose and effect).*
AF7 *(select appropriate and effective vocabulary).*

Speaking and listening
Speaking (speak with clarity, intonation and pace).
Group discussion and interaction (support others, take turns).

Resources

Phase 1
Interactive activity, 'Research'
Photocopiable page, 'Text types' (versions 1 and 2)
Interactive activity, 'Information texts and reports'
Phase 2
Interactive activity, 'Persuasive texts'
Photocopiable page, 'Create an advert' (versions 1 and 2)
Phase 4
Interactive activity, 'Features of reports'
Interactive activity, 'Features of instructions'
Photocopiable page, 'Recounts' (versions 1 and 2)
Periodic assessment
Interactive activity, 'Non-fiction 3 Reading assessment'
Photocopiable page, 'Non-fiction 3 Writing assessment'

Unit 3 ▢ Information texts

Learning outcomes	Assessment opportunity and evidence	Assessment focuses (AFs)		Success criteria
		Level 2	Level 3	
Phase ① activities pages 125-126				
Research • Children can make informed choices for research based on their prior knowledge. • Children can note information collected from a range of sources.	• Supported group activity where children complete an interactive activity to demonstrate their knowledge of research methods and a quick research activity. • Children's completed interactive activity and oral responses.	**Reading AF2** • Some specific, straightforward information recalled. • Generally clear idea of where to look for information.	**Reading AF2** • Simple, most obvious points identified though there may also be some misunderstanding. • Some comments include quotations from or references to text, but not always relevant.	I can describe how to research topics.
Instructions and reports • Children can make informed choices for research based on their prior knowledge. • Children can note information collected from a range of sources.	• Supported group activity where children compare and identify two different types of text. • Children's oral and written responses. • Children's completed photocopiable pages. • Children's responses to the interactive activity.	**Reading AF4** • Some awareness of use of features of organisation.	**Reading AF4** • A few basic features of organisation at text level identified, with little or no linked comment.	• I can recognise the features of reports. • I can recognise the features of instruction texts.
Phase ② activities pages 127-128				
Persuasion Children can recognise the features and purpose of simple persuasive texts.	• Supported paired activity where children discuss and identify persuasive language in an interactive activity. • Children's completed interactive activity and oral responses.	**Reading AF6** • Some awareness that writers have viewpoints and purposes. • Simple statements about likes and dislikes in reading, sometimes with reasons.	**Reading AF6** • Comments identify main purpose. • Express personal response but with little awareness of writer's viewpoint or effect on reader.	I can recognise the features of simple persuasive texts.
Create an advert Children can recognise the features and purpose of simple persuasive texts.	• Supported group activity where children create an advertisement. • Children's written responses and oral evaluations.	**Writing AF7** • Simple, often speech-like vocabulary conveys relevant meanings. • Some adventurous word choices.	**Writing AF7** • Simple, generally appropriate vocabulary used, limited in range. • Some words selected for effect or occasion.	I can create an advertisement.
Phase ④ activities pages 129-131				
Plan and write a report Children can use notes collected from a range of sources and present them in different forms and evaluate their effectiveness.	• Supported paired activity where children undertake an interactive activity to secure knowledge about report writing and plan and write an introduction and a further paragraph. • Children's completed interactive activity. • Children's written responses.	**Reading AF4** • Some awareness of use of features of organisation. **Writing AF5** • Some variation in sentence openings. • Mainly simple sentences with *and* used to connect clauses. • Past and present tense generally consistent.	**Reading AF4** • A few basic features of organisation at text level identified, with little or no linked comment. **Writing AF5** • Reliance mainly on simply structured sentences, variation with support. • *and, but, so* are the most common connectives, subordination occasionally. • Some limited variation in use of tense and verb forms, not always secure.	• I can recognise the features of reports. • I can plan a report. • I can write a report.

Unit 3 📖 Information texts

Learning outcomes	Assessment opportunity and evidence	Assessment focuses (AFs)		Success criteria
		Level 2	Level 3	
Plan and write instructions Children can use notes collected from a range of sources and present them in different forms, including ICT, and evaluate their effectiveness.	• Supported paired activity where children undertake an interactive activity to secure knowledge about instructions and plan and write a set of instructions. • Children's completed interactive activity. • Children's written and oral responses.	**Reading AF4** • Some awareness of use of features of organisation. **Writing AF7** • Simple, often speech-like vocabulary conveys relevant meanings. • Some adventurous word choices.	**Reading AF4** • A few basic features of organisation at text level identified, with little or no linked comment. **Writing AF7** • Simple, generally appropriate vocabulary used, limited in range. • Some words selected for effect or occasion.	• I can recognise the features of instructions. • I can plan and write instructions.
Recounts Children can use notes collected from a range of sources and present them in different forms, including ICT, and evaluate their effectiveness.	• Supported paired activity where children plan and write a recount. • Children's oral evaluations. • Children's written responses.	**Writing AF7** • Simple, often speech-like vocabulary conveys relevant meanings. • Some adventurous word choices.	**Writing AF7** • Simple, generally appropriate vocabulary used, limited in range. • Some words selected for effect or occasion.	• I can plan a recount. • I can write a recount.

Learning outcomes	Assessment opportunity and evidence	Assessment focuses (AFs)		Success criteria
		Level 4	Level 5	
Phase ① activities pages 125–126				
Research • Children can make informed choices for research based on their prior knowledge. • Children can note information collected from a range of sources.	• Independent activity where children complete an interactive activity to demonstrate their knowledge of research methods and a quick research activity. • Children's completed interactive activity and oral responses.	**Reading AF2** • Some relevant points identified. • Comments supported by some generally relevant textual reference or quotation.	**Reading AF2** • Most relevant points clearly identified, including those selected from different places in the text. • Comments generally supported by relevant textual reference or quotation, even when points made are not always accurate.	I can describe how to research topics.
Instructions and reports • Children can make informed choices for research based on their prior knowledge. • Children can note information collected from a range of sources.	• Independent activity where children compare and identify two different types of text. • Children's oral and written responses. • Children's completed photocopiable pages. • Children's responses to the interactive activity.	**Reading AF4** • Some structural choices identified with simple comment. • Some basic features of organisation at text level identified.	**Reading AF4** • Comments on structural choices show some general awareness of writer's craft. • Various features relating to organisation at text level, including form, are clearly identified, with some explanation.	• I can recognise the features of reports. • I can recognise the features of instruction texts.
Phase ② activities pages 127–128				
Persuasion Children can recognise the features and purpose of simple persuasive texts.	• Paired activity where children discuss and identify persuasive language in an interactive activity. • Children's completed interactive activity and oral responses.	**Reading AF6** • Main purpose identified. • Simple comments show some awareness of writer's viewpoint. • Simple comment on overall effect on reader.	**Reading AF6** • Main purpose clearly identified, often through general overview. • Viewpoint in texts clearly identified, with some, often limited, explanation. • General awareness of effect on the reader, with some, often limited, explanation.	I can recognise the features of simple persuasive texts.

Unit 3 ☐ Information texts

Learning outcomes	Assessment opportunity and evidence	Assessment focuses (AFs)		Success criteria
		Level 4	Level 5	
Create an advert Children can recognise the features and purpose of simple persuasive texts.	• Independent activity where children create an advertisement. • Children's written responses and oral evaluations.	**Writing AF7** • Some evidence of deliberate vocabulary choices. • Some expansion of general vocabulary to match topic.	**Writing AF7** • Vocabulary chosen for effect. • Reasonably wide vocabulary used, though not always appropriately.	I can create an advertisement.

Phase ④ activities pages 129–131

Plan and write a report Children can use notes collected from a range of sources and present them in different forms and evaluate their effectiveness.	• Paired activity where children undertake an interactive activity to secure knowledge about report writing and plan and write an introduction and a further paragraph. • Children's completed interactive activity. • Children's written responses.	**Reading AF4** • Some structural choices identified with simple comment. • Some basic features of organisation at text level identified. **Writing AF5** • Some variety in length, structure or subject of sentences. • Use of some subordinating connectives throughout the text. • Some variation, generally accurate, in tense and verb forms.	**Reading AF4** • Comments on structural choices show some general awareness of writer's craft. • Various features relating to organisation at text level, including form, are clearly identified, with some explanation. **Writing AF5** • A variety of sentence lengths, structures and subjects provides clarity and emphasis. • Wider range of connectives used to clarify relationship between ideas. • Some features of sentence structure used to build up detail or convey shades of meaning.	• I can recognise the features of reports. • I can plan a report. • I can write a report.
Plan and write instructions Children can use notes collected from a range of sources and present them in different forms, including ICT, and evaluate their effectiveness.	• Paired activity where children undertake an interactive activity to secure knowledge about instructions and plan and write a set of instructions. • Children's completed interactive activity. • Children's written and oral responses.	**Reading AF4** • Some structural choices identified with simple comment. • Some basic features of organisation at text level identified. **Writing AF7** • Some evidence of deliberate vocabulary choices. • Some expansion of general vocabulary to match topic.	**Reading AF4** • Comments on structural choices show some general awareness of writer's craft. • Various features relating to organisation at text level, including form, are clearly identified, with some explanation. **Writing AF7** • Vocabulary chosen for effect. • Reasonably wide vocabulary used, though not always appropriately.	• I can recognise the features of instructions. • I can plan and write instructions.
Recounts Children can use notes collected from a range of sources and present them in different forms, including ICT, and evaluate their effectiveness.	• Paired activity where children plan and write a recount. • Children's oral evaluations. • Children's written responses.	**Writing AF7** • Some evidence of deliberate vocabulary choices. • Some expansion of general vocabulary to match topic.	**Writing AF7** • Vocabulary chosen for effect. • Reasonably wide vocabulary used, though not always appropriately.	• I can plan a recount. • I can write a recount.

Phase ① Research

Learning outcomes
● Children can make informed choices for research based on their prior knowledge.
● Children can note information collected from a range of sources.

Success criteria
I can describe how to research topics.

Setting the context
This activity should be carried out once the children have been given a topic to research, for example, one related to another area of the curriculum, such as science or geography. They should have discussed what they already know about it and what they need to find out. They should have discussed and identified a variety of research methods in group or whole-class sessions. Children working at levels 2-3 work on the activity in a small group supported by an adult. When the children have completed the interactive activity 'Research' invite them to demonstrate their research abilities by giving them a new topic and asking them to make a note of their prior knowledge and to then quickly find out one new fact about it. Invite children working at levels 4-5 to answer questions on the interactive activity 'Research' independently.

Assessment opportunity
The interactive activity provides an opportunity to assess how secure the children are in their knowledge of the methods to use for researching information on a specific topic. Children working at levels 2-3 work in a supported group and discuss the reasons for their choice of answers with a supporting adult. Children working at levels 4-5 will work independently. When they have completed the activity ask them to give reasons for their choice of answers and explain why they eliminated the remaining two choices.

Assessment evidence
At levels 2-3, children will know how to find specific and straightforward information and they will be able to refer back to the source of reference later if necessary. At levels 4-5, children will be more aware that they may sometimes have to gather information from a variety of sources and a range of reading material of different types. Use your notes on the children's oral responses and the results of the interactive activity to provide evidence towards Reading AF2.

Next steps
Support: Provide children who are still unsure about researching information with a question and three non-fiction texts, one of which is relevant and two which will not provide the answer. Ask them to answer the question and describe the text where they found the answer. Repeat this activity several times with different information sources.
Extension: Provide children with a topic to research and a limited time in which to find the information.

Key aspects of learning
Enquiry: Children will ask questions, research and then plan how to present the information effectively.
Information processing: Children will identify relevant information from a range of sources on paper and on screen.
Communication: Children will often work collaboratively in paired, group and whole-class contexts. They will communicate outcomes orally, in writing and through ICT if appropriate.

NON-FICTION

Phase ① Instructions and reports

Learning outcomes
● Children can make informed choices for research based on their prior knowledge.
● Children can note information collected from a range of sources.

Success criteria
● I can recognise the features of reports.
● I can recognise the features of instruction texts.

Setting the context
This activity should be carried out once the children have explored the language and layout of written instructions and the language and typical features of non-chronological reports. They should have compared the purposes of the text types and discussed which type would be useful when researching information about a topic. Invite the children to demonstrate their ability to recognise the features of each type of text by annotating the photocopiable page 'Text types', and then completing the interactive activity 'Information texts and reports'. Children working at levels 2–3 should work on version 1 of the photocopiable page, while version 2 is suitable for those working at levels 4–5.

Assessment opportunity
Children working at levels 2–3 work in pairs in a supported group on the photocopiable page. An adult can assist the group in identifying the main differences between a report and an instruction text by asking questions to help them identify the key features, for example: *Can you circle the verbs in text 1? Now find the verbs in text 2. How are they different? Does this give you a clue about the type of text?* The supporting adult can make notes of the children's responses on the class list. When the children have annotated and identified the two types of text, invite them to complete the interactive activity independently. Children working at levels 4–5 work independently on the photocopiable page.

Assessment evidence
At levels 2–3, children will identify correctly the relevant organisational features of the different text types. At levels 4–5, children will be able to explain as well as identify these features, commenting on different aspects of the writer's craft – for example, how and why the text is structured as it is. Use the children's written responses, notes made on their comments and the completed interactive activity to provide evidence towards Reading AF4.

Next steps
Support: Revisit appropriate activities from Non-fiction units 1 and 2 for those children who struggled to identify the language features of either text type.
Extension: Provide the children with information books that contain more than one type of text and ask them to identify the different text types.

Key aspects of learning
Information processing: Children will identify relevant information from a range of sources on paper and on screen.
Communication: Children will often work collaboratively in paired, group and whole-class contexts. They will communicate outcomes orally, in writing and through ICT if appropriate.

NON-FICTION

Phase ② Persuasion

Learning outcome
Children can recognise the features and purpose of simple persuasive texts.

Success criteria
I can recognise the features of simple persuasive texts.

Setting the context
This activity should be undertaken after the children have explored the typical language used in simple persuasive texts, for example advertisements and safety advice, in print and on television. They should have explored the purposes of persuasive text, such as to make someone want to buy something or to act in a certain way. Ensure the children understand the ways persuasive texts: grab the reader or viewer's attention, use brief sentences and phrases, ask questions with obvious answers, give brief information using facts and figures or statistics and ask the reader to respond. Invite the children working at levels 4-5 to complete the interactive activity 'Persuasive texts' in pairs. Children working at levels 2-3 work in pairs with a supporting adult.

Assessment opportunity
The children should work in pairs, discussing the sentences on each screen and identifying their purposes as they complete the interactive activity. Ask for feedback about their choices and make notes on the class list. Children working with a supporting adult discuss the sentences with the adult, who can deepen their thinking by asking them what the purpose of the sentence is, for example: *Is it asking you a question? Do you know what the answer is? Why? Is it giving you facts or figures? Why?*

Assessment evidence
At levels 2-3, children will show some awareness that the writer of the text has a particular purpose in mind. However they will not easily understand the more subtle, persuasive texts. At levels 4-5, children will more clearly identify the purpose behind the writer's words. They will be able to explain the writer's viewpoint and comment on how the text affects the reader. Use the children's oral responses and the completed interactive activity to provide evidence towards Reading AF6.

Next steps
Support: Provide children who struggle to recognise persuasive techniques with a selection of paper advertisements from magazines and ask them to highlight the similarities.
Extension: Invite children to evaluate a selection of newspaper advertisements and choose the most effective one, giving reasons for their choice.

Key aspects of learning
Information processing: Children will process information from a range of sources on paper and on screen.
Reasoning: Children will explain their opinion about the effectiveness of simple persuasive texts against agreed success criteria.
Communication: Children will work collaboratively in paired, group and whole-class contexts. They will communicate outcomes orally, in writing and through ICT if appropriate.

Phase ② Create an advert

Learning outcome
Children can recognise the features and purpose of simple persuasive texts.

Success criteria
I can create an advertisement.

Setting the context
This activity should be undertaken when the children have explored the typical language used in a variety of advertisements on paper and on television, through shared, guided and independent work. They should have explored the purposes of persuasive text, such as to make someone want to buy something or to act in a certain way. Ensure the children understand the ways persuasive texts: grab the reader or viewer's attention, use brief sentences and phrases, ask questions with obvious answers, give brief information using facts and figures or statistics and ask the reader to respond. Invite the children working at levels 4–5 to use the photocopiable page 'Create an advert' (version 2) to make note of the language they need to use when creating their own advertisement independently. Others working at levels 2–3 work in a small group on photocopiable page 'Create an advert' (version 1) with a supporting adult and create their advertisement collaboratively. Before beginning the activity, as a class, decide on something to be the subject for the advertisement.

Assessment opportunity
Children working in a supported group can discuss the prompts and collaborate to make choices of language on the photocopiable page. When the activity is complete, ask the children to use their notes to create a polished version. Display the advertisements and ask individuals to choose which they think is the most effective and give reasons for their choices. Children working at levels 4–5 fill in the photocopiable page independently.

Assessment evidence
At levels 2–3, children will use relevant but simple vocabulary, often speech-like, with the occasional more interesting word thrown in. Their sentence structure will also be simple and sometimes repetitive. At levels 4–5, children will make an effort to attract and maintain the reader's interest with vocabulary chosen deliberately for effect. Sentences will vary in structure, bringing clarity and emphasis as necessary. Use the children's notes, the finished advertisements and notes made on the children's oral evaluations to provide evidence towards Writing AF7.

Next steps
Support: Let the children who struggle to create an effective advertisement cut out words and phrases from different newspaper advertisements and rearrange them to create a new advertisement.
Extension: Invite children to create an advertisement on the computer using clip art and different font effects.

Key aspects of learning
Information processing: Children will process information from a range of sources on paper and on screen.
Reasoning: Children will explain their opinion about the effectiveness of simple persuasive texts against agreed success criteria.
Communication: Children will work collaboratively in paired, group and whole-class contexts. They will communicate outcomes orally, in writing and through ICT if appropriate.

Phase ④ Plan and write a report

Learning outcome
Children can use notes collected from a range of sources and present them in different forms and evaluate their effectiveness.

Success criteria
- I can recognise the features of reports.
- I can plan a report.
- I can write a report.

Setting the context
This activity should be undertaken after the children have explored the language and conventions of report texts. They should also be familiar with the final outcome for Unit 3: to create different text types on one topic for a slideshow presentation. The class should have discussed and chosen the topic for their written outcome and researched information to include in a range of texts. Explain that this assessment activity focuses on writing report text. Invite the children to complete the interactive activity 'Features of reports' in pairs.

Assessment opportunity
The children working at levels 2–3 work with a supporting adult. When the activity is complete, ask the children at levels 4–5 to use their research notes to plan and write an introduction in pairs, then to independently write two further paragraphs each for a report. Children working at levels 2–3 work with a supporting adult to plan an introduction and write one further paragraph each. When they have completed the task, ask them to read their reports aloud and evaluate their own writing. Give them the following points on which to base their evaluations: *Does the introduction describe what the report will be about? Do the paragraphs link together? Have you used the present tense consistently? Have you grouped information in paragraphs logically? What one thing are you pleased with? What one thing could you improve?* Children working at levels 4–5 work on the interactive activity independently.

Assessment evidence
At levels 2–3, children will write simple sentences using relevant but generally mundane vocabulary. When reading others' reports they will note the basic organisational features. At levels 4–5, children will write sentences that vary in structure. Their aim is to hold the reader's attention and their vocabulary is chosen deliberately for effect. When evaluating classmates' reports they will comment on how the text is structured and why. Use the completed interactive activity to provide evidence for Reading AF4. Use the plans, final reports and notes on the children's oral evaluations, to provide evidence for Writing AF5.

Next steps
Support: Revisit earlier activities on report text as appropriate for those who are insecure about the layout and language of report text.
Extension: Invite children to write a conclusion to their reports.

Key aspects of learning
Enquiry: Children will ask questions, research and then plan how to present information effectively.
Information processing: Children will process information from a range of sources on paper and on screen.
Social skills: When developing collaborative writing, children will learn to listen to and respect others' viewpoints and take on different roles within a group to complete a task.
Communication: Children will work collaboratively in paired, group and whole-class contexts. They will communicate outcomes orally, in writing and through ICT if appropriate.

NON-FICTION

Phase ④ Plan and write instructions

Success criteria
● I can recognise the features of instructions.
● I can plan and write instructions.

Setting the context
This activity should be undertaken after the children have explored the language and conventions of instruction texts. They should now be familiar with the final outcome for Unit 3: to create different text types on one topic for a slideshow presentation. The class should have discussed and chosen the topic for their written outcome and researched information to include in a range of texts. Explain that this activity focuses on writing instructions. Invite the children to complete the interactive activity 'Features of instructions' in pairs.

Assessment opportunity
Children working at levels 2–3 work with a supporting adult. When the activity is complete, ask those at levels 4–5 to use their research notes to plan and write their instructions together in pairs. Children working with a supporting adult should plan and write their instructions. When they have completed the task, ask them to swap their instructions and evaluate each other's writing. Give them the following points on which to base their evaluations: *Do the instructions have a clear aim and list of what is needed? Are the steps clearly and logically sequenced? Can you understand the instructions?* Children working at levels 4–5 do the interactive activity independently.

Assessment evidence
At levels 2–3, children will write simple instructions using relevant vocabulary, but may sometimes lack the technical terminology needed. When reading others' instructions they will note the basic organisational features. At levels 4–5, children will write clear sentences including relevant technical terms and adverbs that communicate precisely the way in which particular steps are to be taken. When evaluating classmates' reports they will comment on how the text is structured and why. Use the plans, final instructions and notes on the children's oral evaluations, to provide evidence for Writing AF7. Use the completed interactive activity to provide evidence for Reading AF4.

Next steps
Support: Revisit earlier activities on report text as appropriate for children who are insecure about the layout and language of instructions.
Extension: Invite the children to use ICT to write their instructions.

Key aspects of learning
Enquiry: Children will ask questions, research and then plan how to present information effectively.
Information processing: Children will process information from a range of sources on paper and on screen.
Social skills: When developing collaborative writing, children will learn to listen to and respect others' viewpoints and take on different roles within a group to complete a task.
Communication: Children will work collaboratively in paired, group and whole-class contexts. They will communicate outcomes orally, in writing and through ICT if appropriate.

Phase ④ Recounts

Learning outcome
Children can use notes collected from a range of sources and present them in different forms, including ICT, and evaluate their effectiveness.

Success criteria
● I can plan a recount.
● I can write a recount.

Setting the context
This activity should be undertaken after the children have revised the language and conventions of recount text and are familiar with the final outcome for Unit 3: to create different text types on one topic for a slideshow presentation. The class should have discussed and chosen the topic for their written outcome and researched information to include in a range of texts. Explain that this activity focuses on writing recounts.

Assessment opportunity
Children working at levels 2–3 plan their recounts with a supporting adult using the photocopiable page 'Recounts' (version 1) and then write their recounts together in pairs. When they have completed the task, ask them to swap their recounts with another pair and evaluate each other's writing. Give them the following points on which to base their evaluations: *Does the recount use past-tense verbs consistently? Is there a clear beginning, middle and ending? Have time-based connectives been used to sequence the recount? Are there paragraphs to signal a change in time, topic, person and place?* Invite children working at levels 4–5 to use their research notes to plan a recount using the photocopiable page 'Recounts' (version 2), and then write their recounts together in pairs.

Assessment evidence
At levels 2–3, children will write simple sentences that tend to be repetitive in structure and use relevant but simple vocabulary. When reading others' recounts they will note the basic organisational features but make few other comments. At levels 4–5, children will write sentences that vary in structure. Their aim is to hold the reader's attention and their vocabulary is chosen deliberately for effect as well as accuracy. When evaluating classmates' reports they will comment on how the text is structured and why. Use the plans, final recounts and notes on the children's oral evaluations, to provide evidence for Writing AF7.

Next steps
Support: Revisit earlier activities on report text as appropriate for those who are insecure about the layout and language of recounts.
Extension: Invite the children to write their recounts on a computer and add graphics.

Key aspects of learning
Enquiry: Children will ask questions, research and then plan how to present information effectively.
Information processing: Children will process information from a range of sources on paper and on screen.
Social skills: When developing collaborative writing, children will learn to listen to and respect others' viewpoints and take on different roles within a group to complete a task.
Communication: Children will work collaboratively in paired, group and whole-class contexts. They will communicate outcomes orally, in writing and through ICT if appropriate.

Periodic assessment

Reading

Learning outcome
Children can recognise the features and purpose of simple persuasive texts, recounts, non-chronological reports and instructions.

Success criteria
- I can recognise the features of reports.
- I can recognise the features of instructions.
- I can recognise the features of simple persuasive text.
- I can recognise the features of recounts.

Setting the context
This assessment should be undertaken after the children have completed Non-fiction Unit 3 and have become familiar with the purposes of persuasive texts, reports, instructions and recounts and their typical language and layout. Discuss individual children's achievements with them. Ask them to suggest what they found difficult about the work in the unit and what they found easy and compare their responses with the noted comments made by supporting adults.

Assessment opportunity
Invite children to complete the interactive activity 'Non-fiction 3 Reading assessment' independently. This activity provides an opportunity for children to demonstrate their understanding of the different language used in persuasive texts, recounts, non-chronological reports and instructions, and to show their ability to differentiate between them. The children choose the correct answers for four different screens and check their answers interactively.

Assessment evidence
Use the children's completed interactive assessment and notes made on their oral comments to provide evidence towards Reading AF4. At levels 2–3, children will identify correctly the varied language used in different text types and will show an awareness of how they are structured. At levels 4–5, children will more easily identify the purposes of non-fiction texts and why they are organised as they are. They will more readily comment on the features of the texts and will be able to explain how they are fit for purpose. Use this activity as well as examples of children's work throughout this unit to make level judgements for Reading.

Periodic assessment

Writing

Learning outcome
Children can use notes collected from a range of sources and present them in different forms, including ICT, and evaluate their effectiveness.

Success criteria
I can evaluate an ICT presentation.

Setting the context
This assessment should be carried out after the children have completed Non-fiction Unit 3. Collect the work that has been completed during the course of the unit and discuss individual children's achievements with them. Ask them to suggest what they found difficult about the work in the unit and what they found easy. Ask them to work in small groups and view the class or another group's slideshow presentation. Invite them to discuss the effectiveness of this way of displaying their work, which parts worked well and which parts could be improved and how. Provide them with a copy of the photocopiable page 'Non-fiction 3 Writing assessment' on which to write their comments. Children working at levels 2–3 work with a supporting adult. A supporting adult can assist children working at levels 2–3 to view and evaluate the slideshow by asking questions such as: *Is the order of the presentation effective? Are there any texts that you don't understand? How could they be improved? Would the report texts in the slideshow be better with more captions? Why? Do you think there is anything missing?* Children working at levels 4–5 work independently on the sheet.

Assessment opportunity
This end-of-unit activity provides an opportunity for pairs of children to study and evaluate the slideshow presentations against an agreed set of criteria. When they have viewed the presentations and made notes, invite the pairs to give their feedback orally to the class.

Assessment evidence
Use the children's notes and their oral feedback to provide evidence towards Writing AF2. At levels 2–3, children will produce non-fiction writing that is generally fit for purpose. The main features of the form will be present and despite using limited vocabulary, the style of writing will generally be appropriate. At levels 4–5, children will write clearly and consistently, showing an awareness of the needs of readers and attempting to hold their interest throughout. Use this activity as well as examples of children's work throughout this unit to make level judgements for Writing.

NON-FICTION

Name   Date

Text types (1)

■ What types of text are these? Mark up the language and layout features to help you identify each text.

How to make cheese on toast
Ingredients:
One slice of bread   Grated cheese
Brown sauce (optional)

- First turn on the grill.
- Place the slice of toast under the grill for 2–3 minutes until it turns golden brown.
- Turn the bread over and grill the other side.
- Remove the bread and cover the slice with the grated cheese.
- Return it to the grill and cook until the cheese melts and begins to bubble.
- Place the bread and cheese on a plate and add sauce.

Snacks
There are many different snacks to choose from. Some can be bought ready-made and some can be made at home.

Ready-made snacks
Ready-made snacks can be bought in shops, supermarkets, sandwich bars and cafes. Sandwiches are one of the most popular snacks.

Home-made snacks
The cheapest way to have a snack is to make it at home. Sandwiches are quick and easy to make.

Illustration © 2009, Anna Godwin.

Red
Amber
Green

I can recognise the features of reports. ☐

I can recognise the features of instruction texts. ☐

Name _____ Date _____

Create an advert (1)

1. What are you selling? _____

_____

2. Finish the question:

Wouldn't you like to _____

_____

_____

_____ ?

3. Write a sentence about how good it is.

_____

_____

_____

4. Ask another question. _____

_____

_____

_____

5. Finish an instruction:

Buy it _____

_____

_____

_____ !

Red
Amber   I can create an advertisement. ☐
Green

POETRY

UNIT 1 Poems to perform

Literacy objectives

Speak and listen for a wide range of purposes in different contexts

Strand 1 Speaking
- Choose and prepare poems or stories for performance, identifying appropriate expression, tone, volume and use of voice and other sounds.

Strand 3 Group discussion and interaction
- Actively include and respond to all members of the group.

Strand 4 Drama
- Identify and discuss qualities of others' performances, including gesture, action and costume.

Read and write for a range of purposes on paper and on screen

Strand 6 Word structure and spelling
- Spell high and medium frequency words.

Strand 7 Understanding and interpreting texts
- Explore how different texts appeal to readers using varied sentence structures and descriptive language.

Strand 8 Engaging with and responding to texts
- Identify features that writers use to provoke readers' reactions.

Strand 10 Text structure and organisation
- Signal sequence, place and time to give coherence.

Strand 11 Sentence structure and punctuation
- Show relationships of time, reason and cause through subordination and connectives.

Strand 12 Presentation
- Write with consistency in the size and proportion of letters and spacing within and between words, using the correct formation of handwriting joins.
- Develop accuracy and speed when using keyboard skills to type, edit and re-draft.

Key aspects of learning

Self-awareness
- Children will discuss and reflect on their personal responses to the poems read.

Creative thinking
- Children will use creative thinking to extend and consider alternatives to simple poetic forms and create a new poem of their own.

Evaluation
- Children will give feedback to others and judge the effectiveness of their own descriptions.

Social skills
- When working collaboratively, children will listen to and respect other people's ideas. They will undertake a variety of roles in group contexts.

Assessment focuses

Reading
AF4 *(identify and comment on the structure and organisation of texts, including grammatical and presentational features at text level).*
AF5 *(explain and comment on writers' use of language, including grammatical and literary features at word and sentence level).*

Writing
AF1 *(write imaginative, interesting and thoughtful texts).*
AF7 *(select appropriate and effective vocabulary).*

Speaking and listening
Speaking (speak with clarity, intonation and pace).
Group discussion and interaction (support others, take turns).
Drama (plan, perform and evaluate poems for performance).

Resources

Phase 1
Photocopiable page, 'Poems for performance'
Phase 2
Photocopiable page, 'Treasure Trove'
Photocopiable page, 'The Magic Box'
Photocopiable page, 'Language in a list poem' (versions 1 and 2)
Periodic assessment
Photocopiable page, 'Poetry 1 Reading assessment'
Photocopiable page, 'Poetry 1 Writing assessment'

Unit 1 ▢ Poems to perform

Learning outcomes	Assessment opportunity and evidence	Assessment focuses (AFs)		Success criteria
		Level 2	Level 3	
Phase ① activity page 140				
Poems for performance • Children can explain their opinions about a poem by referring to particular words and phrases and the subject of the poem. • Children can identify where language is used to create an effect.	• Supported group activity where children read and discuss two poems. • Children's discussions and oral responses, and notes on the photocopiable.	**Reading AF4** • Some awareness of use of features of organisation.	**Reading AF4** • A few basic features of organisation at text level identified, with little or no linked comment.	• I can identify rhythm, rhyme and repetition in a poem. • I can recognise how the structure of a poem affects performance.
Phase ② activity page 141				
Language in a list poem Children can identify where language is used to create an effect.	• Discussion group activity where children read two poems and decide which they like best and why. • Children's discussions and oral responses in a group. • Individual written responses.	**Reading AF5** • Some effective language choices noted. • Some familiar patterns of language identified. **Writing AF1** • Mostly relevant ideas and content, sometimes repetitive or sparse. • Some apt word choices create interest. • Brief comments, questions about events or actions suggest viewpoint.	**Reading AF5** • A few basic features of writer's use of language identified, but with little or no comment. **Writing AF1** • Some appropriate ideas and content included. • Some attempt to elaborate on basic information or events. • Attempt to adopt viewpoint, though often not maintained or inconsistent.	I can write a list poem.
Phase ③ activity page 142				
Writing a performance poem Children can write a poem that uses language to create an effect.	• Group activity where children use a writing frame to create the rhythm for a poem, collaborate to write words to fit the rhythm and then perform their poem. • Children's discussions and oral responses in a group. • Group written responses.	**Writing AF1** • Mostly relevant ideas and content, sometimes repetitive or sparse. • Some apt word choices create interest. • Brief comments, questions about events or actions suggest viewpoint. **Writing AF5** • Some variation in sentence openings. • Mainly simple sentences with *and* used to connect clauses. • Past and present tense generally consistent. **Writing AF7** • Simple, often speech-like vocabulary conveys relevant meanings. • Some adventurous word choices.	**Writing AF1** • Some appropriate ideas and content included. • Some attempt to elaborate on basic information or events. • Attempt to adopt viewpoint, though often not maintained or inconsistent. **Writing AF5** • Reliance mainly on simply structured sentences, variation with support. • *and, but, so* are the most common connectives, subordination occasionally. • Some limited variation in use of tense and verb forms, not always secure. **Writing AF7** • Simple, generally appropriate vocabulary used, limited in range. • Some words selected for effect or occasion.	I can write and perform poetry.

Unit 1 📖 Poems to perform

Learning outcomes	Assessment opportunity and evidence	Assessment focuses (AFs)		Success criteria
		Level 4	**Level 5**	
Phase ① activity page 140				
Poems for performance ● Children can explain their opinions about a poem by referring to particular words and phrases and the subject of the poem. ● Children can identify where language is used to create an effect.	● Independent activity. ● Children's written comments.	**Reading AF4** ● Some structural choices identified with simple comment. ● Some basic features of organisation at text level identified.	**Reading AF4** ● Comments on structural choices show some general awareness of writer's craft. ● Various features relating to organisation at text level, including form, are clearly identified, with some explanation.	● I can identify rhythm, rhyme and repetition in a poem. ● I can recognise how the structure of a poem affects performance.
Phase ② activity page 141				
Language in a list poem Children can identify where language is used to create an effect.	● Discussion group activity where children read two poems and decide which they like best and why. ● Children's discussions and oral responses in a group. ● Individual written responses.	**Reading AF5** ● Some basic features of writer's use of language identified. ● Simple comments on writer's choices. **Writing AF1** ● Relevant ideas and content chosen. ● Some ideas and material developed in detail. ● Straightforward viewpoint generally established and maintained.	**Reading AF5** ● Various features of writer's use of language identified, with some explanation. ● Comments show some awareness of the effect of writer's language choices. **Writing AF1** ● Relevant ideas and material developed with some imaginative detail. ● Development of ideas and material appropriately shaped for selected form. ● Clear viewpoint established, generally consistent, with some elaboration.	I can write a list poem.
Phase ③ activity page142				
Writing a performance poem Children can write a poem that uses language to create an effect.	● Group activity where children use a writing frame to create the rhythm for a poem, collaborate to write words to fit the rhythm and then perform their poem. ● Children's discussions and oral responses in a group. ● Group written responses.	**Writing AF1** ● Relevant ideas and content chosen. ● Some ideas and material developed in detail. ● Straightforward viewpoint generally established and maintained. **Writing AF5** ● Some variety in length, structure or subject of sentences. ● Use of some subordinating connectives throughout the text. ● Some variation, generally accurate, in tense and verb forms. **Writing AF7** ● Some evidence of deliberate vocabulary choices. ● Some expansion of general vocabulary to match topic.	**Writing AF1** ● Relevant ideas and material developed with some imaginative detail. ● Development of ideas and material appropriately shaped for selected form. ● Clear viewpoint established, generally consistent, with some elaboration. **Writing AF5** ● A variety of sentence lengths, structures and subjects provides clarity and emphasis. ● Wider range of connectives used to clarify relationship between ideas. ● Some features of sentence structure used to build up detail or convey shades of meaning. **Writing AF7** ● Vocabulary chosen for effect. ● Reasonably wide vocabulary used, though not always appropriately.	I can write and perform poetry.

POETRY

Phase ① Poems for performance

Learning outcomes
- Children can explain their opinions about a poem by referring to particular words and phrases and the subject of the poem.
- Children can identify where language is used to create an effect.

Success criteria
- I can identify rhythm, rhyme and repetition in a poem.
- I can recognise how the structure of a poem affects performance.

Setting the context
This activity should be carried out once the children have been taught to perform a poem and have had practice at identifying poetic devices typical of performance poetry, such as strong rhythm, rhyme and wordplay. More confident learners may be aware of the term 'alliteration'. Read the two poems from the photocopiable page 'Poems for performance' to the children: 'It's Not What I'm Used To' by Jan Dean and 'Where Do All the Teachers Go?' by Peter Dixon. Explain that they are to read both poems and decide which would make a good performance poem. Children working at levels 2-3 work in a supported discussion group. Questions a supporting adult might ask to draw out responses could include: *Which poem has the stronger rhythm? Which poem is divided into short verses? Can you find the rhyming words in both poems? Which one would sound better performed by a group? Why do you think that?* Children working at levels 4-5 independently annotate the poems.

Assessment opportunity
Children working at levels 2-3 will work in a discussion group supported by an adult. Read both poems once, then read 'It's Not What I'm Used To'. Ask the children to identify any verses and find the rhymes and repetition. Emphasise the rhythm and identify any alliteration. Mark up the pages with their ideas while making a note of the children's contributions. Repeat with the second poem 'Where Do All the Teachers Go?'. Children working at levels 4-5 will work independently on the photocopiable page 'Poems for performance' and compare rhyme, rhythm, structure and any other poetic devices and mark them on the sheets.

Assessment evidence
At levels 2-3, children will identify the most basic features of rhyme, rhythm and structure while you annotate the text. Children at levels 4-5 will mark up the poem independently. They will show some insight into the effects of the features identified and will be able to give reasons for their choice of one poem as being the best suited to performance. Use the children's comments and completed photocopiable pages as evidence for Reading AF4. (The presentation of 'It's Not What I'm Used To' might also provide evidence towards AF5.)

Next steps
Support: For those children who could not identify the rhythm in 'Where Do All the Teachers Go?', select several poems with strong rhythms and clap the rhythm out as you read them together.
Extension: Challenge pairs of children to read through poetry anthologies and select poems with strong rhythm and repetition to perform to the rest of the class.

Key aspects of learning
Self awareness: Children will discuss and reflect on their personal responses to poems read.
Social skills: When working collaboratively, children will listen to and respect other people's ideas. They will undertake a variety of roles in group contexts.

Phase ② Language in a list poem

Learning outcome
Children can identify where language is used to create an effect.

Success criteria
I can write a list poem.

Setting the context
Provide the children with copies of 'Treasure Trove' by Irene Rawnsley and 'The Magic Box' by Kit Wright from the photocopiable pages. Allow the children time to read and analyse the use of unusual images in both poems. The poems provide the opportunity for assessing the children's understanding of the effect of placing mundane, everyday images and magical images together by poets.

Assessment opportunity
Give the children sufficient time to read the poems, to digest them and to decide which they liked best and why. In small discussion groups, of similar ability, the children express their preferences and explain their reasons for them. Before asking questions, to encourage extra depth, allow the children time to discuss their thoughts between themselves. Record their comments. Ask: *Which poem created the most powerful images? Which list was the most effective? Where in both poems do the poets group an ordinary image with something surprising or unusual? What effect did each poem have on you?* Provide the children with the writing frame from the photocopiable page 'Language in a list poem' and ask them to write three verses of a list poem. Children working at levels 2–3 use version 1 of the page, and those at levels 4–5 use version 2. Some children may add one line to each verse, others may add a second.

Assessment evidence
At level 2 and above, children will identify their preference for a particular poem; those working at levels 4–5 will give reasons for their choice, perhaps identifying unusual images such as *spiders wrapped in bandages* or *a cowboy on a broomstick*. Use these comments as evidence for Reading AF5. At levels 2–3, children should produce appropriate ideas and content, though this might be repetitive and sparse. At levels 4–5, children will develop and elaborate their ideas with more imaginative detail and a more consistent poetic voice. Use the children's list poems as evidence for Writing AF1.

Next steps
Support: Choose appropriate poems to send home, with questions to lead children who struggled to recognise unusual imagery in a poem. Examples are: 'If Only I Were' by Shanta Acharya, 'Amazing Inventions' by James Carter.
Extension: Select a poem each week for children to take home, read and analyse and then to share and discuss in class. Keep this up as a regular end-of-week or start-of-week activity.

Key aspects of learning
Reasoning: Children will identify, explore and generate the mental connections represented by various forms of simple imagery – for example, simile – a vital aspect of thinking, reasoning and understanding.
Self-awareness: Children will discuss and reflect on their personal responses to the poems.
Communication: Children will develop their ability to discuss effective communication in respect of both the language and content of poetry they are reading and writing. They will sometimes work collaboratively in pairs and groups. They will communicate outcomes orally, and in writing (possibly using ICT).

POETRY

Phase ③ Writing a performance poem

Learning outcome
Children can write a poem that uses language to create an effect.

Success criteria
I can write and perform poetry.

Setting the context
This activity should be carried out after the children have spent a week studying performance poetry. They should have examined a variety of performance poems and explored the use of strong rhythm and rhyme as well as the use of imagery and alliteration.

Assessment opportunity
Provide the children with a writing frame, based on one of the poems they have been studying, using a limited number of lines and verses. Include an opening line to set the rhythm and give them a starting point for working on rhyme. In small groups, encourage the children to clap the rhythm of the opening line and to collaborate to work out an idea of how the rhythm will continue through the poem. Ask the children to suggest how to continue the poem and note down words and phrases to use. Allot one child or an adult to scribe for the group as they collaborate on writing the performance poem. Record which children make active contributions to the group. Each group can then perform their finished poem together.

Assessment evidence
At levels 2–3, children will use simple vocabulary, with an occasional word selected for effect. They will use the simplest connectives and there will be little variety in their writing. Most of their ideas will be relevant and some children may try to establish a clear poetic voice. Children working at levels 4–5 will use varied and exciting vocabulary, deliberately chosen for effect and variety and to establish detail and meaning. The poetic voice will be clearer and more consistent. Use your notes on children's contributions to provide evidence for Writing AF1, AF5 and AF7.

Next steps
Support: For those who struggled to recognise the rhythm of the opening line and continue it through the poem, provide a daily poem and ask them to clap the rhythm with a partner rather than in a group; for those who struggled to contribute to the group collaboration, run a similar activity in pairs on several occasions before reassessing in pairs.
Extension: Children write their own performance poems on topics of their choice independently.

Key aspects of learning
Social skills: When working collaboratively, children will listen to and respect other people's ideas. They will undertake a variety of roles in group contexts.
Reasoning: Children will explore and generate rhythm and rhyming vocabulary.

■SCHOLASTIC

Periodic assessment

Reading

Learning outcomes

● Children can explain their opinions about a poem by referring to particular words and phrases and the subject of the poem.
● Children can identify where language is used to create an effect.

Success criteria

I can identify how the language in a poem is creating an effect.

Setting the context

This assessment should be carried out once the children have completed Poetry Unit 1. Give the children a copy of the photocopiable page 'Poetry 1 Reading assessment' and ask them to answer the seven questions about the poem, 'Fairy Picnic' by Peter Dixon. The question types range from literal (about the subject and rhyme), to deductive (how the focus of the verses differ), to evaluative (about the whole poem). Read the poem aloud to the children before providing them with their copy and the questions. Ask them to re-read the poem carefully. Tell them to annotate any poetic features they find in the poem before reading the questions. Explain that doing this will help them to answer the questions as well as they can.

Assessment opportunity

The children should be given sufficient time to allow them to read and digest the poem and to annotate it before answering the questions. This activity provides an opportunity to assess the children's ability to understand and analyse a previously unseen poem and answer questions to demonstrate their understanding of the use of poetic language and their appreciation of the poem as a whole. Go through the responses of children working at levels 2–3 orally, allowing them to expand on their written answers.

Assessment evidence

Use the annotated poems and written responses to provide evidence for Reading AF5 and AF6. At levels 2–3, children will express likes and dislikes but with limited awareness of the writer's viewpoint. They will be aware of features and patterns in the poem, but may not appreciate their effects. At levels 4–5, children will be more aware of the writer's viewpoint and will better understand the effects on the reader of the language and the poetic techniques used (for example, rhyme and alliteration). Use this activity as well as examples of children's work throughout this unit to make level judgements for Reading.

POETRY

Periodic assessment

Writing

Learning outcome
Children can write a poem that uses language to create an effect.

Success criteria
I can write and perform poetry.

Setting the context
This assessment should be carried out once the children have completed Poetry Unit 1. Remind the children about some of the unusual and effective images in the list and other performance poetry they have read, for example, *A marble full of dragon smoke* from 'Treasure Trove' by Irene Rawnsley; *Three violet wishes* from 'The Magic Box' by Kit Wright. Provide the children with copies of the photocopiable page 'Poetry 1 Writing assessment'. Invite them to write a list poem based around the things they keep in their bedrooms. Encourage them to make notes of words, phrases and unusual images to use before they begin.

Assessment opportunity
Ask the children to collaborate with a partner to create their list poem and then perform it for others in the class. This provides an opportunity to assess their ability to work together and to create effective list poems. Some children may include rhythm, rhyme or unusual combinations of vocabulary to create effective images. Encourage other children in the class when listening to the poems to describe two effective uses of language and performance for each poem. Notes could be made of the children's evaluations of the poems.

Assessment evidence
Use the poetry written during Unit 1 and on the photocopiable page 'Poetry 1 Writing assessment' - together with your notes about each child's awareness of the poetic strengths of others - to provide evidence for Writing AF1 and AF7. Children working at levels 2-3 will include some appropriate content in their writing, using some of the poetic devices listed. However their attempts to elaborate will be limited. They will appreciate in others' work the more adventurous vocabulary chosen. Children working at levels 4-5 will produce relevant, detailed and imaginative content, reinforced by the poetic devices listed and they will establish a clear and consistent poetic voice. Use this activity as well as examples of children's work throughout this unit to make level judgements for Writing.

Poems for performance

It's Not What I'm Used To

I don't want to go to Juniors . . .

The chairs are too big.
I like my chair small, so I fit
Exactly
And my knees go
Just so
Under the table.

And that's another thing –
The tables are too big.
I like my table to be
Right
For me
So my workbook opens
Properly.
And my pencil lies in the space at the top
The way my thin cat stretches into a long line
On the hearth at home.

Pencils – there's another other thing.
Another problem.
    Up in Juniors they use pens and ink.
     I shall really have to think
      About ink.

Jan Dean

Poem © 2005, Jan Dean (2005, Macmillan). Illustration © 2009, Anna Godwin.

POETRY

Poems for performance

Where Do All the Teachers Go?

Where do all the teachers go
When it's 4 o'clock?
Do they live in houses
And do they wash their socks?

Do they wear pyjamas
And do they watch TV?
And do they pick their noses
The same as you and me?

Do they live with other people
Have they mums and dads?
And were they ever children
And were they ever bad?

Did they ever, never spell right
Did they ever make mistakes?
Were they punished in the corner
If they pinched the chocolate flakes?

Did they ever lose their hymn books
Did they ever leave their greens?
Did they scribble on the desk tops
Did they wear old dirty jeans?

I'll follow one back home today
I'll find out what they do
Then I'll put it in a poem
That they can read to you.

Peter Dixon

Poem © 1998, Peter Dixon (1998, Macmillan). Illustration © 2009, Anna Godwin.

POETRY

Treasure Trove

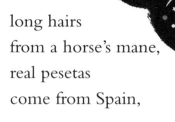

I have a tin
to keep things in
underneath
my bedroom floor.

I put my finger
in the crack,
quietly lift
the floorboard back,

and there's my store,
safely hid
in a tin with roses
on the lid.

A few feathers
and a chicken's claw,
a big tooth
from a dinosaur,

the wrapper
from my Easter Egg,
a Christmas robin
with one leg,

long hairs
from a horse's mane,
real pesetas
come from Spain,

three of my
operation stitches,
like spiders
wrapped in bandages,

a marble
full of dragon smoke,
flashing with fire
in the dark,

a magic pebble
round and white,
a sparkler left
from bonfire night.

Underneath
my bedroom floor
there's a treasure tin,
with my things in.

Irene Rawnsley

POETRY

UNIT 2 Shape poems and calligrams

Literacy objectives

Speak and listen for a wide range of purposes in different contexts
Strand 1 Speaking
● Sustain conversation, explain or give reasons for their views or choices.

Read and write for a range of purposes on paper and on screen
Strand 6 Word structure and spelling
● Spell high and medium frequency words.
● Recognise a range of prefixes and suffixes, understanding how they modify meaning and spelling, and how they assist in decoding long, complex words.
● Spell unfamiliar words using known conventions including grapheme-phoneme correspondences and morphological rules.
Strand 7 Understanding and interpreting texts
● Explore how different texts appeal to readers using varied sentence structures and descriptive language.
Strand 8 Engaging with and responding to texts
● Identify features that writers use to provoke readers' reactions.
Strand 9 Creating and shaping texts
● Make decisions about form and purpose, identify success criteria and use them to evaluate their writing.
● Use layout, format, graphics and illustrations for different purposes.
Strand 11 Sentence structure and punctuation
● Compose sentences using adjectives, verbs and nouns for precision, clarity and impact.
Strand 12 Presentation
● Write with consistency in the size and proportion of letters and spacing within and between words, using the correct formation of handwriting joins.
● Develop accuracy and speed when using keyboard skills to type, edit and re-draft.

Key aspects of learning

Reasoning
● Children will explain their opinion about different poems, using particular words and phrases to support or illustrate their ideas.
Creative thinking
● Children will have the opportunity to respond imaginatively to the stimulus of a first-hand experience and may be able to express their response through music, art or dance before writing poems.
Evaluation
● Children will have regular opportunities to review their written work against agreed success criteria.
Communication
● Children will develop their ability to discuss aspects of poetry and poetic language as they work collaboratively in paired, group and whole-class contexts. They will communicate outcomes orally, in writing and through ICT if appropriate.

Unit 2 Shape poems and calligrams

Assessment focuses

Reading
AF5 *(explain and comment on writers' use of language, including grammatical and literary features at word and sentence level).*
AF6 *(identify and comment on writers' purposes and viewpoints, and the overall effect of the text on the reader).*

Writing
AF1 *(write imaginative, interesting and thoughtful texts).*
AF7 *(select appropriate and effective vocabulary).*

Speaking and listening
Speaking (speak with clarity, intonation and pace).

Resources

Phase 1
Photocopiable page, 'Shapes'
Phase 2
Photocopiable page, 'Creating similes' (versions 1 and 2)
Interactive activity, 'Creating similes'
Periodic assessment
Photocopiable page, 'Poetry 2 Reading assessment'

Unit 2 ◻ Shape poems and calligrams

Learning outcomes	Assessment opportunity and evidence	Assessment focuses (AFs)		Success criteria
		Level 2	Level 3	
Phase ① activities pages 152–153				
Shapes Children can explain what they like about a poem by referring to particular words and phrases and the subject of the poem.	● Paired activity where children appraise a shape poem and compare it with others they have read before and appraise each other's responses. ● Paired evaluations of the responses to the poem on the photocopiable page. ● Children's annotations and written responses.	**Reading AF6** ● Some awareness that writers have viewpoints and purposes. ● Simple statements about likes and dislikes in reading, sometimes with reasons.	**Reading AF6** ● Comments identify main purpose. ● Express personal response but with little awareness of writer's viewpoint or effect on reader.	I can read and compare shape poems.
Calligrams Children can write a calligram, choosing appropriate presentational features using ICT to create effects and can describe why these effects have been chosen.	● Independent activity where children explore different word-art and font effects using ICT and choose the best effects for each word to create a calligram. ● Printed and hand-written evidence.	**Writing AF1** ● Mostly relevant ideas and content, sometimes repetitive or sparse. ● Some apt word choices create interest. ● Brief comments, questions about events or actions suggest viewpoint.	**Writing AF1** ● Some appropriate ideas and content included. ● Some attempt to elaborate on basic information or events. ● Attempt to adopt viewpoint, though often not maintained or inconsistent.	I can write a calligram.
Phase ② activity page 154				
Creating similes ● Children can identify examples where language is used to create a specific effect in a poem. ● Children can discuss the choice of words and their impact.	● Discussion group and independent activity where children identify the similes in a poem, then describe the image a simile generates and invent similar similes. ● Children's oral, written and interactive responses.	**Reading AF6** ● Some awareness that writers have viewpoints and purposes. ● Simple statements about likes and dislikes in reading, sometimes with reasons. **Writing AF7** ● Simple, often speech-like vocabulary conveys relevant meanings. ● Some adventurous word choices.	**Reading AF6** ● Comments identify main purpose. ● Express personal response but with little awareness of writer's viewpoint or effect on reader. **Writing AF7** ● Simple, generally appropriate vocabulary used, limited in range. ● Some words selected for effect or occasion.	I can create poetic words and phrases.
Phase ③ activity page 155				
Creating a shape poem Children write a poem collaboratively that uses language to create an effect.	● Supported group activity where children collaborate to create a shape poem. ● The class display of completed shape poems.	**Writing AF7** ● Simple, often speech-like vocabulary conveys relevant meanings. ● Some adventurous word choices.	**Writing AF7** ● Simple, generally appropriate vocabulary used, limited in range. ● Some words selected for effect or occasion.	I can create a shape poem.

Unit 2 ◻ Shape poems and calligrams

Learning outcomes	Assessment opportunity and evidence	Assessment focuses (AFs)		Success criteria
		Level 4	Level 5	
Phase ① activities pages 152-153				
Shapes Children can explain what they like about a poem by referring to particular words and phrases and the subject of the poem.	• Paired evaluations of the responses to the poem on the photocopiable page. • Children's annotations and written responses.	**Reading AF6** • Main purpose identified. • Simple comments show some awareness of writer's viewpoint. • Simple comment on overall effect on reader.	**Reading AF6** • Main purpose clearly identified, often through general overview. • Viewpoint in texts clearly identified, with some, often limited, explanation. • General awareness of effect on the reader, with some, often limited, explanation.	I can read and compare poems.
Calligrams Children can write a calligram, choosing appropriate presentational features using ICT to create effects and can describe why these effects have been chosen.	• Independent activity where children explore different word-art and font effects using ICT and choose the best effects for each word to create a calligram. • Printed and hand-written evidence.	**Writing AF1** • Relevant ideas and content chosen. • Some ideas and material developed in detail. • Straightforward viewpoint generally established and maintained.	**Writing AF1** • Relevant ideas and material developed with some imaginative detail. • Development of ideas and material appropriately shaped for selected form. • Clear viewpoint established, generally consistent, with some elaboration.	I can write a calligram.
Phase ② activity page 154				
Creating similes • Children can identify examples where language is used to create a specific effect in a poem. • Children can discuss the choice of words and their impact.	• Independent activity where children identify the similes in a poem, then describe the image a simile generates and invent similar similes. • Children's written and interactive responses.	**Reading AF6** • Main purpose identified. • Simple comments show some awareness of writer's viewpoint. • Simple comment on overall effect on reader. **Writing AF7** • Some evidence of deliberate vocabulary choices. • Some expansion of general vocabulary to match topic	**Reading AF6** • Main purpose clearly identified, often through general overview. • Viewpoint in texts clearly identified, with some, often limited, explanation. • General awareness of effect on the reader, with some, often limited, explanation. **Writing AF7** • Vocabulary chosen for effect. • Reasonably wide vocabulary used, though not always appropriately.	I can create poetic words and phrases.
Phase ③ activity page 155				
Creating a shape poem Children write a poem collaboratively that uses language to create an effect.	• Collaborative activity where children create a shape poem. • The class display of completed shape poems.	**Writing AF7** • Some evidence of deliberate vocabulary choices. • Some expansion of general vocabulary to match topic	**Writing AF7** • Vocabulary chosen for effect. • Reasonably wide vocabulary used, though not always appropriately.	I can create a shape poem.

Phase ① Shapes

Learning outcome
Children can explain what they like about a poem by referring to particular words and phrases and the subject of the poem.

Success criteria
I can read and compare shape poems.

Setting the context
This activity should be carried out after the children have spent time reading and exploring the effect of several varied shape poems. The children work in pairs and read a different poem each. They annotate the poem by highlighting words and phrases that they like and answer the questions about it at the bottom of the page. They then swap poems with each other and read their partner's appraisal of the poem.

Assessment opportunity
This activity provides an opportunity for children to assess each other's responses to a shape poem. The poem is 'Inside' by James Carter. Each child has the opportunity to appraise the poem and write a summary of the effects of the poem's shape and subject matter that they like on the photocopiable page 'Shapes'. They are also asked to compare the poem with others they have read before. The children then swap with a partner and the partner appraises the other's responses by finding two comments they think are good, and one they think could be improved.

Assessment evidence
At levels 2–3, children will be able to state, in simple terms, what they like and dislike about the chosen poem. However they will not be able to describe the effects on the reader; neither will they comment on the poetic voice. At levels 4–5, children will be able to elaborate on why the poet chose particular devices (such as the poem's shape), and will describe with more insight the effects on the reader (in this case, surprise, sympathy, identifying with the poet). Use this activity as evidence towards Reading AF6.

Next steps
Support: For those who struggled to find any features in the poem that appealed to them, find another shape poem that they already like and ask them to describe the features that make this poem appealing and compare it with the poem on the photocopiable page 'Shapes'.
Extension: Send a shape poem home and ask the children to appraise it for homework.

Key aspects of learning
Self-awareness: Children reflect on their personal responses to poems read.
Reasoning: Children will explain their responses to different poems, using particular words and phrases to support or illustrate their ideas.
Creative thinking: Children will have the opportunity to respond imaginatively to the stimulus and express their response.
Evaluation: Children will evaluate and give feedback to others on their shape poems.

Phase ① Calligrams

Learning outcome
Children can write a calligram, choosing appropriate presentational features using ICT to create effects and can describe why these effects have been chosen.

Success criteria
I can write a calligram.

Setting the context
This activity should be carried out after the children have spent some time reading and exploring how different fonts and shapes of words can be used in poetry to reflect the meaning of words. Some examples of calligrams to use, taken from *Word Whirls and Other Shape Poems* compiled by John Foster (Oxford University Press, 1998) are: 'Umbrella' by Catherine Benson, 'Holiday Memories' by Paula Edwards, 'Rhythm Machine' by Trevor Harvey. The children should have had the opportunity to explore how to portray the meanings of various adjectives, nouns and verbs through action and movement. Provide them with three words of your choosing, for example: *freezing, frightening, shrinking.* Working independently, the children explore different word-art and font effects using ICT and choose the best effects for each word to create a calligram.

Assessment opportunity
This activity provides an opportunity to assess the children's understanding of the meanings of words and how to reflect that meaning through manipulating fonts on a computer. The children try out three different font effects for each word. They save each example as they experiment to find the best effect to reflect the meaning of the word. Print off the children's work and discuss the different effects they have used. Ask them to tell you which calligram is the best for each of the three words. The children then write a sentence on their document to say which their final choices are and why they chose each of them.

Assessment evidence
At levels 2–3, children will include some relevant content and apt choices of vocabulary, however the poetic voice may be inconsistent. At levels 4–5, children will be better able to match the content, ideas and voice to the poem's shape, forming a cohesive whole. The vocabulary chosen will be both relevant and imaginative and there will be more detailed development of particular ideas. Use the children's work to provide evidence for Writing AF1.

Next steps
Support: Give other examples of calligrams to those children who struggled to create an imaginative interpretation of the words and ask them to recreate them using pen and paper.
Extension: Children use their best calligrams to write a poem of their own.

Key aspects of learning
Self-awareness: Children reflect on their personal responses to poems read.
Reasoning: Children will explain the reasons for their choices of best calligram.
Creative thinking: Children will have the opportunity to respond imaginatively to the stimulus and express their response.
Evaluation: Children will evaluate their own work and give reasons for their choice of final outcome when writing a calligram.

Phase ② Creating similes

Learning outcomes
● Children can identify examples where language is used to create a specific effect in a poem.
● Children can discuss the choice of words and their impact.

Success criteria
I can create poetic words and phrases.

Setting the context
This activity should be carried out after the children have been taught the definition of a simile and have had practice identifying them in a variety of poems. More confident learners may be aware of the terms 'metaphor' and 'personification'. Before running the activity, ensure the children are able to define a simile as a way of drawing a comparison by using 'like' or 'as' to create an image for the reader. The children analyse a poem of your choosing, in which the poet uses a number of similes to create images. An example is the poem 'Canary' by Jan Dean. Read the poem aloud to the children and ask them to tell you what the poem is about before they begin work. Using the photocopiable page 'Creating similes', they begin by identifying all the similes. Children working at levels 2-3 work on version 1 of the page, and those at levels 4-5 use version 2. Ask the children to underline and number the similes and describe their effects. They then write another simile that could be used to similar effect. The children then move on to the interactive activity 'Creating similes'.

Assessment opportunity
This activity provides an opportunity to assess the children's understanding of how poets use similes to create an image in the reader's mind. Children working at levels 2-3 will work first in a discussion group before identifying the similes. Read a verse, then ask questions to check if the children can identify similes: *To what is the poet comparing the canary's skull? Why do you think the poet chose this simile?* (To show how fragile it is.) *To what is the poet comparing the canary's body?* (Sunshine in a box.) *Why do you think the poet chose this simile?* (Shutting sunshine in a box might make readers feel sad.) *Can you think of another simile that would have a similar effect?* Children working at levels 4-5 will work independently on the poem, which will show whether they can identify similes and explain why the poet chose the language to create those images.

Assessment evidence
At levels 2-3, children will identify similes and will understand that the poet has a purpose in using them; in discussion, they will express their own preferences. The similes they write themselves will be simple and of limited effectiveness. At levels 4-5, children will understand the poet's purpose in using a particular simile and will also be aware of its impact on readers. The similes they write will contain deliberate choices of imagery and the logic behind their comparisons will be more accessible to readers. Use the children's appreciation of similes as evidence for Reading AF6; use the similes they write as evidence for Writing AF7.

Next steps
Support: Those children who could not explain why the language was used to create the specific images, work on creating similes of their own in small discussion groups. Provide them with an object or pictures and ask them to draw comparisons, asking: *What does it look like? What does it feel like?* and so on.
Extension: Challenge children to read through poetry anthologies and select poems containing language which creates images. Invite them to write up the poem and comment on it, and stick it in a class anthology of favourite poems. The children then share their choices with the class.

Key aspects of learning
Self-awareness: Children reflect on their personal responses to poems read.
Reasoning: Children will explain their opinions about poetic language and its effects.
Creative thinking: Children will have the opportunity to respond imaginatively to the stimulus and express their response.

Phase ③ Creating a shape poem

Learning outcome
Children write a poem collaboratively that uses language to create an effect.

Success criteria
I can create a shape poem.

Setting the context
This activity should be carried out after the children have been taught the definition of a simile and have had practice identifying them in a variety of poems and writing their own. Before running the activity, ensure the children are able to define a simile as a way of drawing a comparison by using 'like' or 'as' to create an image for the reader. Groups of children are provided with a large outline shape of something from a topic they have been reading about and a piece of paper each. Suitable outlines might be an animal shape (for example, a tiger, a snake, a snail), a tree or flower shape or similar. In a group, children think of and discuss comparisons for the outline shape and then independently write a simile each on their paper. They cut out their similes and, as a group, experiment with the order of the similes to create the best effect. The children then glue their similes in order inside the outline shape.

Assessment opportunity
This activity provides an opportunity to assess the children's understanding of how poets use similes to create an image in the reader's mind. Children working at levels 2–3 will work first in a supported group before writing their own similes and then as a group, arranging them inside the outline shape. The adult supporting the group asks questions to stimulate the children's imaginations, such as: *How does the tiger move? What does it look like? Give me a simile that says this, for example, the tiger moves as silently as…'.* Children working at levels 4–5 will work collaboratively on the task.

Assessment evidence
At levels 2–3, children will write simple poems that may include the occasional adventurous and effective idea. Their similes will be simple and of limited effectiveness. At levels 4–5, children will be more innovative. Their similes will contain deliberate choices of imagery and the logic behind their comparisons will be more accessible to readers. The children's outline shape poems can be displayed and used to provide evidence for Writing AF7.

Next steps
Support: Encourage children who struggle to create imaginative similes to look through poetry anthologies to find poems that use similes and make a collection of the similes they like most.
Extension: Challenge children to write another shape poem independently using language to create images.

Key aspects of learning
Reasoning: Children will explain their opinions about shape poems using particular words and phrases to illustrate their ideas.
Creative thinking: Children will have the opportunity to respond imaginatively to the stimulus and express their response.

POETRY

Periodic assessment

Reading

Learning outcome
Children can explain what they like about a poem by referring to particular words and phrases and the subject of the poem.

Success criteria
I can read and compare shape poems.

Setting the context
This assessment should be carried out once the children have completed Poetry Unit 2. The children are given a copy of two poems, 'Autumn' by Tony Langham and 'Cat Dream' by Catherine Benson, on the photocopiable page 'Poetry 2 Reading assessment'. They answer five questions about the subject and form of both poems and make evaluative judgements about them, stating their preferences with reasons. Read the poems aloud to the children before providing them with their own copy and the questions. Ask them to look closely at the forms of both poems and tell them to re-read them carefully. Tell them to annotate any interesting features they find in the poems before reading the questions. Explain that doing this will help them to answer the questions as well as they can.

Assessment opportunity
The children should be given sufficient time to allow them to read and digest the poems and to annotate them before answering the questions. This activity provides an opportunity to assess the children's ability to understand and analyse two previously unseen shape poems and answer questions to demonstrate their understanding of the use of poetic language and their ability to state a preference with supporting reasons.

Assessment evidence
The children's annotations and written responses will provide evidence for Reading AF5 and AF6. Go through these orally with the children working at levels 2–3, allowing them to expand on and explain their answers. They will identify the basic poetic features of the two poems and make simple comparisons between them. However they will find it difficult to comment on these features or to explain their own preferences. Children working at levels 4–5 will be better able to compare the poems and to identify their effects on the reader. They will also identify and understand the main purpose of each poem. Use this activity as well as examples of children's work throughout this unit to make level judgements for Reading.

Periodic assessment

Writing

Learning outcome
Children can write a calligram, choosing appropriate presentational features using ICT to create effects, and can describe why these effects have been chosen.

Success criteria
I can write a calligram.

Setting the context
This assessment should be carried out once the children have completed Poetry Unit 2. Remind the children about some of the unusual and effective uses of shape and letters in calligram poetry they have read. Provide the children with a list of nouns, verbs, adjectives and adverbs. Invite them to choose a word from the list and use word-processing software to create a calligram, changing size, shape and colour to create the best effects. Words you could use for them to select from could include: *shivery, cold, hot, melting, fast, wobbly, growth, growing, muddled, shaky, large, small, jump, slippery* and so on.

Assessment opportunity
This provides an opportunity to assess children's understanding of how calligrams use font effects, shape and size to reflect the meaning or image of the words they represent. Children working at levels 2-3 could work with a supporting adult to stimulate their imaginations in their use of font effects. The completed calligrams can be printed off and displayed and used to provide evidence for Writing AF1 and AF2.

Assessment evidence
The children's responses and the poetry they have written earlier in Unit 2 will provide evidence for Writing AF1 and AF2. At levels 2-3, children will use some appropriate poetic features and may take account of some of the needs of the reader. At levels 4-5, children will be consistent in poetic style and will aim to hold the reader's attention with imaginative detail. A clear, poetic voice helps to ensure that the content remains relevant. Use this activity as well as examples of children's work throughout this unit to make level judgements for Writing.

Name   Date

Shapes

■ Read the poem and circle any words and phrases or lines that you like. In the margin, write why you like these words and phrases.

Inside

Now
you
may think
I'm walking tall
I'm talking big
I've got it all –
but here inside
I'm ever so shy
I sometimes cry
I'm curled in a ball
I'm no feet small
no   I'm
not   big
not   tall
at   all

James Carter

1. What is the poem about?

_____

_____

2. What is your favourite line and why?

_____

_____

PHOTOCOPIABLE ■SCHOLASTIC

Poem © 2005, James Carter (2005, Pan Macmillan).

3. Why is this poem written in this shape?

_____

_____

_____

4. Do you like this poem more or less than another you have read? Explain your answer.

_____

_____

_____

5. Ask your partner to complete this part and write his/her name underneath:

Two things your partner did really well.

1: _____

_____

2: _____

_____

One thing they could improve.

_____

_____

_____

Red
Amber   I can read and compare shape poems. ☐
Green

POETRY

Poetry 2 Reading assessment

■ Read the two poems and answer the questions.

Cat Dream

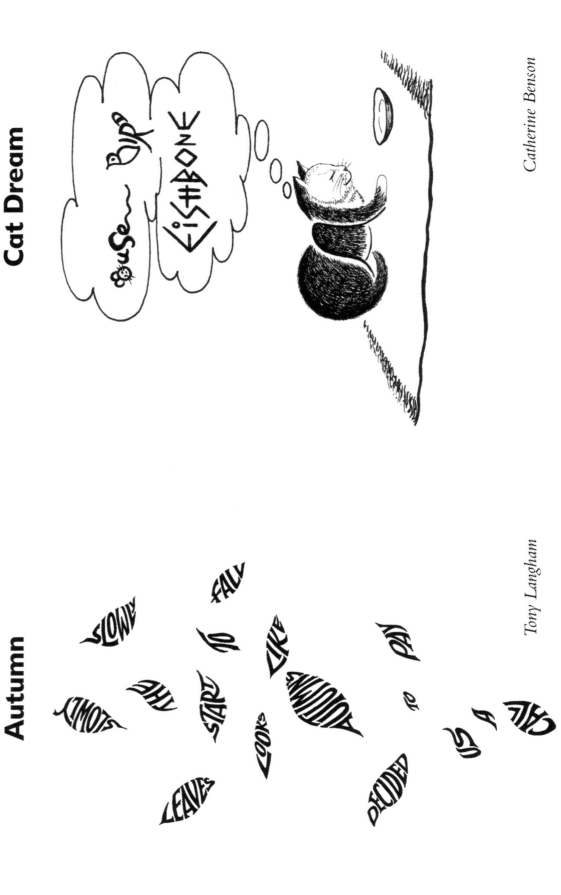

Catherine Benson

Autumn

Tony Langham

Unit 2 🔲 **Shape poems and calligrams**

1. Which poem uses rhyme?

_____

2. Write the rhyming words.

_____

_____

3. In the poem 'Autumn', what effect has the poet created with shape?

_____

_____

4. In the poem 'Cat Dream', how does the poet write the words 'mouse', 'bird' and 'fishbone'?

_____

_____

5. Which poem do you prefer and why?

_____

_____

_____

_____

_____

_____

_____

_____

_____

Red

Amber   I can read and compare shape poems. ☐

Green

POETRY
UNIT 3 Language play

Literacy objectives

Speak and listen for a wide range of purposes in different contexts
Strand 1 Speaking
- Choose and prepare poems or stories for performance, identifying appropriate expression, tone, volume and use of voices and other sounds.
- Sustain conversation, explain or give reasons for their views or choices.

Read and write for a range of purposes on paper and on screen
Strand 7 Understanding and interpreting texts
- Explore how different texts appeal to readers using varied sentence structures and descriptive language.
Strand 8 Engaging with and responding to texts
- Identify features that writers use to provoke readers' reactions.
Strand 9 Creating and shaping texts
- Select and use a range of technical and descriptive vocabulary.
- Use layout, format, graphics and illustrations for different purposes.
Strand 11 Sentence structure and punctuation
- Compose sentences using adjectives, verbs and nouns for precision, clarity and impact.
Strand 12 Presentation
- Write with consistency in the size and proportion of letters and spacing within and between words, using the correct formation of handwriting joins.
- Develop accuracy and speed when using keyboard skills to type, edit and re-draft.

Key aspects of learning

Reasoning
- Children will explain their opinion about different poems, using particular words and phrases to support or illustrate their ideas.
Creative thinking
- Children will have the opportunity to respond imaginatively to the stimulus of a first-hand experience and may be able to express their response through music, art or dance before writing poems.
Evaluation
- Children will have regular opportunities to review their written work against agreed success criteria.

Assessment focuses

Reading

AF5 *(explain and comment on writers' use of language, including grammatical and literary features at word and sentence level).*

AF6 *(identify and comment on writers' purposes and viewpoints, and the overall effect of the text on the reader).*

Writing

AF1 *(write imaginative, interesting and thoughtful texts).*

AF3 *(organise and present whole texts effectively, sequencing and structuring information, ideas and events).*

AF7 *(select appropriate and effective vocabulary).*

Speaking and listening:

Speaking (speak with clarity, intonation and pace).

Resources

Phase 1
Photocopiable page, 'Rhyming couplets'
Interactive activity, 'Rhyming couplets'
Phase 2
Photocopiable page, 'Tongue-twisters' (versions 1 and 2)
Periodic assessment
Photocopiable page, 'Poetry 3 Reading assessment'
Photocopiable page, 'Poetry 3 Writing assessment'

POETRY

Learning outcomes	Assessment opportunity and evidence	Assessment focuses (AFs)		Success criteria
		Level 2	Level 3	
Phase ① activity page 166				
Rhyming couplets Children can identify where language is used to create a specific effect in a poem.	● Supported activity where children read a poem and select a rhyming word to complete the poem. ● Completed photocopiable pages and notes made on children's responses.	**Reading AF5** ● Some effective language choices noted. ● Some familiar patterns of language identified.	**Reading AF5** ● A few basic features of writer's use of language identified, but with little or no comment.	I can write rhyming couplets.
Phase ② activity page 167				
Alliterative phrases ● Children can identify examples where language is used to create a specific effect in a poem. ● Children can discuss the choice of words and their impact.	● Paired activity where children select words from a given list to create alliterative tongue-twisters. ● Children's completed photocopiable pages and notes made on children's responses.	**Reading AF5** ● Some effective language choices noted. ● Some familiar patterns of language identified. **Writing AF7** ● Simple, often speech-like vocabulary conveys relevant meanings. ● Some adventurous word choices.	**Reading AF5** ● A few basic features of writer's use of language identified, but with little or no comment. **Writing AF7** ● Simple, generally appropriate vocabulary used, limited in range. ● Some words selected for effect or occasion.	● I can write alliterative phrases. ● I can play with words.
Phase ③ activity page 168				
Acrostic poems ● Children can write a poem that uses language to create an effect. ● Children can discuss the choice of words and their impact.	● Independent activity where children write an acrostic poem using imaginative adjectives and evaluate each other's poems. ● Children's completed poems and notes made on children's responses.	**Reading AF6** ● Some awareness that writers have viewpoints and purposes. ● Simple statements about likes and dislikes in reading, sometimes with reasons. **Writing AF7** ● Simple, often speech-like vocabulary conveys relevant meanings. ● Some adventurous word choices.	**Reading AF6** ● Comments identify main purpose. ● Express personal response but with little awareness of writer's viewpoint or effect on reader. **Writing AF7** ● Simple, generally appropriate vocabulary used, limited in range. ● Some words selected for effect or occasion.	I can write an acrostic poem.

Learning outcomes	Assessment opportunity and evidence	Assessment focuses (AFs)		Success criteria
		Level 4	Level 5	
Phase ① activity page 166				
Rhyming couplets Children can identify where language is used to create a specific effect in a poem.	● Independent activity where children read a poem and select a rhyming word for each couplet to complete the poem. ● Children's completed photocopiable pages and notes made on children's responses.	**Reading AF5** ● Some basic features of writer's use of language identified. ● Simple comments on writer's choices.	**Reading AF5** ● Various features of writer's use of language identified, with some explanation. ● Comments show some awareness of the effect of writer's language choices.	I can write rhyming couplets.

Unit 3 Language play

Learning outcomes	Assessment opportunity and evidence	Assessment focuses (AFs)		Success criteria
		Level 4	Level 5	
Phase ② activity page 167				
Alliterative phrases • Children can identify examples where language is used to create a specific effect in a poem. • Children can discuss the choice of words and their impact.	• Paired activity where children either select words from a given list or choose their own words to create alliterative tongue-twisters. • Completed photocopiable pages and notes made on children's responses.	**Reading AF5** • Some basic features of writer's use of language identified. • Simple comments on writer's choices. **Writing AF7** • Some evidence of deliberate vocabulary choices. • Some expansion of general vocabulary to match topic.	**Reading AF5** • Various features of writer's use of language identified, with some explanation. • Comments show some awareness of the effect of writer's language choices. **Writing AF7** • Vocabulary chosen for effect. • Reasonably wide vocabulary used, though not always appropriately.	• I can write alliterative phrases. • I can play with words
Phase ③ activity page 168				
Acrostic poems • Children can write a poem that uses language to create an effect. • Children can discuss the choice of words and their impact.	• Independent activity where children write an acrostic poem using imaginative adjectives and evaluate each other's poems. • Children's completed poems and notes made on children's responses.	**Reading AF6** • Main purpose identified. • Simple comments show some awareness of writer's viewpoint. • Simple comment on overall effect on reader. **Writing AF7** • Some evidence of deliberate vocabulary choices. • Some expansion of general vocabulary to match topic.	**Reading AF6** • Main purpose clearly identified, often through general overview. • Viewpoint in texts clearly identified, with some, often limited, explanation. • General awareness of effect on the reader, with some, often limited, explanation. **Writing AF7** • Vocabulary chosen for effect. • Reasonably wide vocabulary used, though not always appropriately.	I can write an acrostic poem.

POETRY

Phase ① Rhyming couplets

Learning outcome
Children can identify where language is used to create a specific effect in a poem.

Success criteria
I can write rhyming couplets.

Setting the context
This activity should be carried out after the children have explored poems with strong, regular rhyming patterns. Before running the activity, ensure the children are able to hear and recognise pairs of rhyming words. Provide children working at levels 2-3 with the photocopiable page 'Rhyming couplets', containing the poem 'Lullaby' by Sue Cowling. Ask the children to select the correct missing rhyming words from the word box and write them into the correct line of the poem. The children then identify one rhyming couplet in the poem that they think uses the most effective language, give a reason for their choice and give an opinion about the use of rhyme in the poem. Children working at levels 4-5 should work on the interactive activity where there are more missing words to fill in.

Assessment opportunity
This activity provides an opportunity to assess the children's ability to hear and generate rhymes and their understanding of how poets use rhyme for effect. Children working at levels 2-3 read the poem and then select a rhyming word for alternate couplets on the photocopiable page. Children working at levels 4-5 work independently to complete the interactive activity 'Rhyming couplets'. Mask the word box on the photocopiable page for more confident learners, before providing the page, and challenge them to fill in the missing rhymes with words of their own. Ask the children to read their chosen rhyming couplet aloud and give a reason for their choice. On the class list, record which children could give reasons for their choice of favourite couplet.

Assessment evidence
At levels 2-3, children will identify the rhymes and provide an additional rhyming word as asked; they will choose a favourite couplet, but will not explain their preference for it. At levels 4-5, children will fill in the blanks with words that rhyme. They will also explain the effects of their favourite couplet and why they like it. The children's completed work provides evidence for Reading AF5.

Next steps
Support: Provide children who struggle to recognise rhyming words with a poem a day to read that has strong rhythm and rhyme. Send the poem home and ask them to read it aloud to someone else, for example, 'Barry's Budgie... Beware!' by David Harmer; 'The Christening Gift' by Sue Cowling; 'Fire at Night' by Andrew Fusek Peters.
Extension: Provide children with a first line and challenge them to write another line to create a rhyming couplet.

Key aspects of learning
Reasoning: Children will explain their opinions about poems using particular words and phrases to support or illustrate their ideas.
Communication: Children will develop their ability to discuss aspects of poetry and poetic language. They will communicate orally, in writing and through ICT if appropriate.

Phase ② Alliterative phrases

Learning outcomes
● Children can identify examples where language is used to create a specific effect in a poem.
● Children can discuss the choice of words and their impact.

Success criteria
● I can write alliterative phrases.
● I can play with words.

Setting the context
This activity should be carried out after the children have been exploring tongue-twisters that are the result of alliterative phrases and sentences, for example, 'Peter Piper picked a peck of pickled pepper'; 'She sells sea shells…'; 'A Fly and a Flea in a Flue…', and other forms of poetry that use alliteration. Provide the children with the photocopiable page 'Tongue-twisters' (versions 1 and 2). Version 1 is suitable for those working at levels 2–3, and version 2 for those at levels 4–5. Individually, the children write a phrase or a sentence making use of alliteration to make a tongue-twister for each of the five names. They can select words from a list or choose words of their own. They then swap their tongue-twisters with a partner who reads them aloud and evaluates the tongue-twisters' success. The partner then writes down two things that were done well and one that could be improved.

Assessment opportunity
This activity provides an opportunity to assess the children's ability to recognise words which begin with the same or similar sounds and put them together to create the best effect. Children working at levels 4–5 may be able to select words from their own knowledge to improve their tongue-twisters. It also provides an opportunity to assess the children's ability to peer-assess other children's work and to give reasons for their opinions. Ask the pairs of children to choose the best tongue-twister their partner has written, read it aloud and say why they chose it. Observe and record notes on which children could explain the reason for their choice of a favourite.

Assessment evidence
At levels 2–3, children will select some appropriate words to write tongue-twisters that make sense. In writing their own tongue-twisters, children working at the higher levels 4–5 will also be able to add appropriate words of their own. Use the children's work as evidence for Writing AF7 and Reading AF5.

Next steps
Support: Encourage children who struggle to choose words with the same initial phonemes to collect alliterative pairs of words when reading other poetry and stories in shared and independent reading.
Extension: Challenge children to write tongue-twisters for their own names and those of other members of the class.

Key aspects of learning
Reasoning: Children will explain their opinions using particular words and phrases to support or illustrate their ideas.
Creative thinking: Children will have the opportunity to respond imaginatively to a stimulus and express their response in writing and orally.
Evaluation: Children will have the opportunity to review their own and other children's work against agreed success criteria.
Communication: Children will develop their ability to discuss aspects of poetry and poetic language. They will communicate orally, in writing and through ICT if appropriate.

POETRY

Phase ③ Acrostic poems

Learning outcomes
● Children can write a poem that uses language to create an effect.
● Children can discuss the choice of words and their impact.

Success criteria
I can write an acrostic poem.

Setting the context
This activity should be carried out after the children have been taught about acrostic poetry and been exposed to a variety of rhyming and non-rhyming acrostics. Write up a non-rhyming acrostic poem on the board to demonstrate, for example, 'Message on the Table' by David Kitchen, which uses the initial letters of each line to give a secret message. Alternatively, create an acrostic based on your own name in a modelled writing session prior to running the activity. Ask the children to write their names vertically down the left side of a piece of paper. Then ask them to choose two adjectives for each letter of their name to describe themselves to make an acrostic poem that also gives a character sketch. Children working at levels 4–5 may choose more than two adjectives.

Assessment opportunity
This activity provides an opportunity to assess the children's ability to choose imaginative adjectives and put them together to create the best poetic effect. It also provides an opportunity to assess the children's abilities to evaluate each other's poems and choice of poetic words. The children take turns to read their acrostic poem aloud to the class. Ask for comments from the other children and make notes on the class list. Record notes on which children could explain the reason for their choice of a favourite.

Assessment evidence
At levels 2–3, children will produce simple acrostics. At levels 4–5, children will also be able to add appropriate words of their own. Use the children's work as evidence for Writing AF7 and Reading AF6.

Next steps
Support: Do the activity again on a later occasion for those children who struggle to find imaginative vocabulary from their own knowledge, and encourage them to use dictionaries and a thesaurus to find interesting adjectives.
Extension: Challenge children to write longer acrostic poems with complete sentences using the names of other class members. They could use ICT as appropriate.

Key aspects of learning
Reasoning: Children will explain their opinions using particular words and phrases to support or illustrate their ideas.
Creative thinking: Children will have the opportunity to respond imaginatively to a stimulus and express their response in writing and orally.
Evaluation: Children will have the opportunity to review their own and other children's work against agreed success criteria.
Communication: Children will develop their ability to discuss aspects of poetry and poetic language. They will communicate orally, in writing and through ICT if appropriate.

Periodic assessment

Reading

Learning outcome
Children can recognise how poets use language to create a vivid picture in words.

Success criteria
I can identify how the language in a poem creates images.

Setting the context
This assessment should be carried out after the children have completed Poetry Unit 3. Give the children a copy of photocopiable page 'Poetry 3 Reading assessment', where they are asked ten questions about the poem 'Summer Farm' by Gareth Owen. The question types range from literal (about the subject, rhyme, alliteration and use of similes), to deductive (how the focus of the verses differs), to evaluative (about the whole poem and powerful images). Read the poem aloud to the children before providing them with their own copy of the photocopiable page. Ask them to re-read the poem carefully. Tell them to annotate any poetic features they find in the poem before reading the questions. Explain that doing this will help them to answer the questions as well as they can.

Assessment opportunity
The children should be given sufficient time to allow them to read and digest the poem and to annotate it before answering the questions. This activity provides an opportunity to assess the children's ability to understand and analyse a previously unseen poem and answer questions to demonstrate their understanding of the use of poetic language and their appreciation of the poem as a whole.

Assessment evidence
Use the children's work as evidence towards Reading AF5 and AF6. At levels 2-3, children will be able to answer the literal questions but will have difficulty with the evaluative questions (8 and 9). At levels 4-5, children will be more able to give reasons for their own responses to the poem and are more likely to show some awareness of the purpose of the poem and the viewpoint of the poet. Use this activity as well as examples of children's work throughout this unit to make level judgements for Reading.

Periodic assessment

Writing

Learning outcome Children can write poems that use poetic images in different forms.	**Success criteria** I can write two different poems that use poetic images for effect.

Setting the context
This assessment should be carried out after the children have completed Poetry Unit 3. Collect the poems the children have written during the course of the unit and allow them time to review their writing and choose one or two of their poems that they feel were the most successful. Provide them with photocopiable page 'Poetry 3 Writing assessment' and explain that they should complete both poems. Allow them time to read the task and give them thinking time before they begin. Let the children make rough notes of ideas on paper. For those working at levels 2-3, go through both of the poetic forms to ensure the children thoroughly understand the different forms.

Assessment opportunity
When the children are reviewing their poetry written during the unit, take the opportunity to ask them to explain their choices about their most successful writing and make notes to provide evidence of self-assessment. The activity using the photocopiable page provides the opportunity to assess the children's ability to make informed choices about their writing and to work to their strengths as poets.

Assessment evidence
Use the children's completed task from the photocopiable page, and the poetry they have written earlier in the unit, as evidence towards Writing AF1 and AF7 and AF8. The poems written by the children working at levels 2-3 will include relevant ideas and content, usually expressed using simple vocabulary; however, there will be little attempt to elaborate on these ideas. Their spelling of high-frequency words will usually be accurate. Those written by children working at levels 4-5 will develop some ideas in more detail, establish a clear, poetic voice and use more original and adventurous vocabulary. They will spell correctly all regular words including those with more than one morpheme. Use this activity as well as examples of children's work throughout this unit to make level judgements for Writing.

Name	Date

POETRY

Rhyming couplets

Lullaby

If I could write some music for the rain

To play upon your nursery window pane

You'd sleep the sounder for its _____

And it would sing more tunefully than I.

If I could teach the clock to tell you tales

Of unicorns and ships with silver _____

You'd never hear the story fail and die

For clocks don't tend to nod as much as I.

If I could knit the shadows into shawls

Unpick bad dreams and wind them into _____

We'd throw them through the window at the sky

Then pull the darkness round us, you and I.

Sue Cowling

Missing words

lullaby   sails   balls

Red
Amber
Green

I can write rhyming couplets. ☐

Name	Date

Poetry 3 Reading assessment

◧ Read the poem 'Summer Farm' then answer the questions about it.

Summer Farm

The mud cakes dry in the farmyard
The clouds have died a death
The lane shimmers like water
The air is holding its breath.

The dogs fall asleep to the music
Of cruising bumble bees
And the cows stand still as statues
As the stream slides past their knees.

Gareth Owen

1. What is the poem describing?

_____

_____

2. Which words rhyme?

_____

_____

3. How many similes are there in the poem?

_____

Poem © 2000, Gareth Owen. Illustration © 2009, Anna Godwin.

Unit 3 Language play

POETRY

4. Write down each simile.

5. How many alliterative phrases are there?

6. Write down each alliterative phrase.

7. How do the first and second verses differ from each other?

8. Do you like or dislike this poem?

9. Write a reason for your answer to question 8.

10. Choose your favourite image from the poem and say why you like it.

Red Amber Green

I can identify how the language in a poem creates images.

SCHOLASTIC PHOTOCOPIABLE

100 LITERACY ASSESSMENT LESSONS · YEAR 3 173

🔲 Transitional assessment

Activity	Type	Level	Description
2.1	Reading comprehension	2	30-minute two-part test based on a narrative extract from *The Snow Lambs* by Debbie Gliori and the poem 'Weather at Work' by Jenny Morris
2.1	Shorter writing task	2	15 minutes; writing a report about different kinds of weather
2.1	Longer writing task	2	30 minutes; writing a recount based on personal experience of problem weather
3.1	Reading comprehension	3	30-minute two-part test based on narrative extracts from *The Sheep Pig* by Dick King-Smith and a non-fiction leaflet for a farm visitors' centre
3.1	Shorter writing task	3	15 minutes; writing an imaginative description of a special pet
3.1	Longer writing task	3	30 minutes; writing letter to persuade the teacher to take the class on a trip to a farm
4.1	Reading comprehension	4	40-minute two-part test based on extracts from *Street Child* by Berlie Doherty and an historical account about Dr Barnardo
4.1	Shorter writing task	4	20 minutes; writing a report on how a typical day in the classroom has changed since the 19th century
4.1	Longer writing task	4	40 minutes; writing imaginative recounts for Dr Barnardo's diary
5.1	Reading comprehension	5	40-minute two-part test based on non-fiction articles on healthy eating and two poems, 'My brother is making a protest about bread' by Michael Rosen and 'Oh, I wish I'd looked after me teeth' by Pam Ayres
5.1	Shorter writing task	5	20 minutes; writing a leaflet to explain 'Good Health Day'
5.1	Longer writing task	5	40 minutes; writing a cautionary tale about healthy eating

NB There are two transitional assessments provided for each level. Transitional tests and tasks 2.2, 3.2, 4.2 and 5.2 are not shown here. All tests and tasks are available on the CD-ROM.

Reading tests: instructions

There are two reading comprehension tests provided at each level (levels 2–5) on the CD-ROM. Each reading test is divided into two parts.

Administering the test
- Allow 30 minutes for both parts of the test at levels 2 and 3, and 40 minutes at levels 4 and 5.
- Children should work unaided.
- Do not read questions or words to them.

Equipment for each child:
- Pencil, eraser (or children may cross out mistakes).

Marking and levelling the children
- Mark the test using the Reading Mark Scheme provided on CD-ROM.
- Add together the marks from both parts of the reading tests (possible total of 30 marks).
- Use the levelling grid at the end of the Mark Scheme to level the test.
- When awarding an end-of-year Teacher Assessment Level, you will also need to consider a child's performance during Periodic and Day-to-Day Assessments. If a child has achieved a low level 3 or above in the transitional tests, it can be assumed that they have achieved AF1 at that level.

Writing tasks: instructions

There are two writing tasks provided at each level (levels 2–5) on the CD-ROM. Each writing task is divided into two parts: shorter and longer writing tasks.

Administering the tasks
Shorter writing task

Allow 15 minutes for each task at levels 2 and 3, and 20 minutes for each task at levels 4 and 5.

Longer writing task

Allow 30 minutes for each task, which could include 5 minutes planning time at levels 2 and 3. Allow 40 minutes for each task, which could include 10 minutes planning time at levels 4 and 5.
- Children should sit so that they cannot see each other's work.
- You may read the task to the children; do not explain the task or help them.
- The task may be administered to groups of children or to the whole class.
- Do not allow children to use dictionaries or word books.

Equipment for each child:
- Pencil, eraser (or children may cross out mistakes) and sheets of plain paper.

Introducing the writing tasks
Say to the children:

I am going to ask you to do some writing.

I will read the task to you, but I cannot help you with your ideas.

If you make a mistake, you should cross it out (or rub it out neatly) and write your word clearly.

Spell the words as best you can, building them up as you usually do.

Marking and levelling the children
- Mark each piece of writing separately using the Writing Mark Scheme, Table 1, provided on the CD-ROM.
- Double the marks gained for the longer Writing task and add this total to the mark gained for the shorter Writing task.
- Assess spelling and handwriting across both pieces of writing using Table 2, provided on the CD-ROM.
- Add the total gained from Table 1 to the total from Table 2.
- Use the grid at the end of the Mark Scheme to find a level for each child.